FILET
CROCHET
TO WEAR

Beginner-friendly patterns
for filet crochet clothes

Lauren Willis

DAVID & CHARLES

www.davidandcharles.com

CONTENTS

THE PROJECTS

INTRODUCTION

Having been a craft dabbler my whole life, I finally turned fully to crochet in my early thirties. I tried knitting but I made too many mistakes and found it impossible to fix them. I dipped my toes in the cross-stitch pool, but those teeny tiny details weren't for me. I even tried the most aggressive of the yarn crafts, needle felting, but I just couldn't get those facial features right! I settled on crochet when I managed to make my first ever blanket (a corner-to-corner chunky make that has since been donated to the dogs) and by the spring of 2020 I was a competent beginner. When lockdown began and my dog grooming business was shut down for a while, I embraced the hook as a way to keep my hands busy.

As much as I enjoy making quick projects, I really love the meditative process of working away on something big and repetitive while watching the television or listening to a podcast in the garden. As soon as I started on my first filet project, I knew it was perfect for me. It needed just enough of my attention that I didn't quickly become bored with it, but not so much attention that I couldn't focus on my box set. I didn't even mind being on sleeve island!

It started with the Time After Time and Festive Firs sweaters. Creating cute little icons within crochet was a revelation to me, and they're still two of my all-time favourite makes. I then began experimenting with texture, combining twisted and touchable stitches with filet in repeating, geometric patterns.

Fast forward a couple of years and a lot of patterns, and here we are enjoying filet crochet together. I hope you find plenty to keep you busy within these pages and that these patterns bring you as much joy as they do me.

Lauren

TOOLS & MATERIALS

Yarn

Throughout this book I have chosen to use Paintbox Yarns. I love the variety of colours available and the durability of the product for a budget-friendly but high-quality make. You can easily swap to your favourite brand of yarn if you prefer, just make sure that you swatch before starting a project. If your gauge (tension) is off with a different yarn it'll make a huge difference to the fit of your garment, and no one wants to waste hours of their time making something ill fitting! See Key Information: Gauge (Tension) for more details.

Crochet hooks

When it comes to hooks, it is best to try out several different types to find the one that suits you. You can use any of your preferred hooks for the projects, although personally I always use a brightly coloured polymer clay hook – mostly because pretty tools make me smile! Shown below is one of the hooks I have used throughout this book, all of which were made by Cupcake Crochet Crafts. I use my 4mm (US size G/6) hook for all the DK (light worsted) yarn projects, but you'll occasionally need a 5mm (US size H/8) for aran (worsted) yarn makes, or a 5.5mm (US size I/9) or 6mm (US size J/10) for edging.

Other tools

Although you're not instructed within the patterns to use stitch markers, they're always useful to have on hand in case you need a little help keeping track. You can mark the first stitch of every row so you know where your final stitch of the next row needs to sit. This will prevent you from accidentally adding or losing stitches. They're also really useful when seaming; you will need to use them to mark where the base of your sleeves will meet your body panels. I also like using them to keep my sleeve in place as I seam – you can anchor your sleeve to your body panels with a few markers to make sure it doesn't move as you seam, which would give you an uneven join (see General Techniques: Finishing, Seaming).

You'll also need to keep a tape measure nearby to check your gauge (tension) as you work. Mine can change dramatically depending on my mood; my Monday morning stitches rarely match those of my Saturday night! Checking your tension occasionally throughout your make will help to ensure that the item fits you perfectly when done.

Once you have your hooks, markers, tape measure and yarn, all you'll need is a pair of scissors for snipping your ends and you'll be ready to get started!

KEY INFORMATION

In the following few pages you will find some important information that will help you to make the perfect filet garment! At the end of the book see the General Techniques section, which explains how to work all the basic and special stitches you will be using.

Colour choice

The colours you choose for your projects will make a huge difference to the finished look of your garments. I originally made Echo Beach in bright yellow and it is easily one of my favourite-ever makes. When I chose the colours for the book, I went for a more muted blue for this one, and it feels like a completely different sweater to me! Time After Time would look amazing in a bright magenta, and Festive Firs looks completely different when made in a soft pastel with bright star details. Don't feel tied to colour choices by what you see in the book – let your imagination go wild and make yourself something new in a daring, attention-grabbing colour.

Look closely at the patterns within the fabric of your chosen make. What do they remind you of? Do the shells and bobbles within Ocean Drive make you think of pebbles in the ocean? Do you like the versatile neutral beige of the Billie Jean Boatneck, or does its simplicity inspire you to go with a bright colour? Let yourself be inspired by the make!

Gauge (tension)

My stitches do tend to be very tight and very tall. If you can meet the given tension for your stitches but not your rows, don't worry too much. Always get as close to the stitch tension as you can because this will make a huge difference to the finished fit of your piece. The majority of the patterns in the book are length adjustable, so it's not always crucial to meet the row tension.

As Paintbox yarns have been used throughout the book, you'll see the tension is always either 16 sts x 9 rows to 10cm (4in) with DK (light worsted) yarn, or 13 sts x 7 rows to 10cm (4in) with aran (worsted) yarn. If you have too few stitches and rows in your swatch, try using a smaller hook. If you have too many, try a larger hook. If you struggle to get your tension just right, think about the fit you would like for your finished make instead. If your bust is 102cm (40¼in) and you're making the Time After Time sweater, you could make the size M for approx. 8cm (3in) positive ease, or for an oversized fit, make the L which would give you around 20cm (8in) positive ease. However, if your tension is a little tighter than mine, you know you will have less ease, so would be better off sizing up to the size L to make sure you don't end up with a sweater which makes you feel suffocated.

ABBREVIATIONS

bead st	bead stitch
beg	begin
BLO	back loop only
BPdc	back post double crochet
CC	contrast colour
ch	chain
cont	continu(e)ing
dc	double crochet
dc2tog	double crochet 2 stitches together
fdc	foundation double crochet
FLO	front loop only
foll	follow(ing)s
FPdc	front post double crochet
hdc	half double crochet
MC	main colour
prev	previous
rem	remaining
rep	repeat
RS	right side
sc	single crochet
sc2tog	single crochet 2 stitches together
sk	skip
sp	space
ss	slip stitch
tog	together
WS	wrong side
yo	yarn over
* *	rep pattern instructions from * to * as many times as stated
[ ]	rep stitch instructions between square brackets as many times as stated

CHART SYMBOLS

⬭	chain
✕	single crochet
⊤	half double crochet
⊤	double crochet
⋈	crossed double crochet
⧓	bead stitch
⬡	bobble
▢	no stitch

STITCH TERMINOLOGY

The patterns in this book are all written in US crochet terminology

US	UK
double crochet (dc)	treble crochet (tr)
foundation dc (fdc)	foundation tr (ftr)
half double crochet (hdc)	half treble crochet (htr)
single crochet (sc)	double crochet (dc)
yarn over (yo)	yarn round hook (yrh)

Sizing

All the patterns have a sizing table at the start and are graded for ten sizes, from XXS (suitable for tweenagers) up to 5X (158cm/62in bust/chest). The sizes include positive ease – extra cm/in allowed so the garment will not be tightly fitting – but this varies between patterns and styles: most of the sweaters are designed with approx. 10–15cm (4–6in) of positive ease for a relaxed fit, but not all the patterns have the same finished measurements due to the stitch repeats used. Once you know your own bust measurement you can decide which size to make based on the fit you would like to achieve. If you would prefer a roomier sweater you can make the next size up to give yourself some extra space, or you could size down for less ease. Most patterns are length adjustable by simply working additional or fewer repeats. Sleeve depth measurements are also given, so you can work the sleeve size that suits you best – for instance, if you're making a size S but want extra room in your sleeves, follow the instructions for the size L sleeves throughout.

There is no reason for any of the makes here to be worn only by women – the bust measurements work for everyone! Simply take your chest measurement (or that of the lucky person you're making for) and work the size that it sits closest to. Now there is no excuse for the whole gang not to be in matching handmade Christmas sweaters.

Adjusting patterns

Most of the sweaters and cardigans have ribbed cuffs as I love them that way, but if you prefer a more open sleeve, work your first row or round to have the same number of stitches as after the cuff increase. For example, if you're making the Silver Linings Sweater in a size L, rather than chain 30 and working your cuff, chain 66 (your stitch count after increasing in Round 7), work one round of double crochet (UK treble crochet), then skip right ahead to Round 8 where the filet pattern begins and work until your sleeve is the desired length. You could even work additional rounds of double crochet and fold your sleeve up for a bulky, rolled cuff.

The same goes for necklines. If you're not a fan of a tight neck on your clothing, you can work a round of double or single crochet (UK treble or double) in place of any ribbing. Trust your instincts – you don't always have to stick exactly to the patterns. That's the beauty of making your own clothes. And if it doesn't work? Simply undo it and try again. Enjoy the creative process!

TO FIT SIZE TABLE

Size	XXS	XS	S	M	L
To fit bust	68–71cm (26–28in)	71–76cm (28–30in)	81–86cm (32–34in)	91–96cm (36–38in)	101–106cm (40–42in)

Size	XL	2X	3X	4X	5X
To fit bust	111–117cm (44–46in)	122–127cm (48–50in)	132–137cm (52–54in)	142–147cm (56–58in)	152–158cm (60–62in)

FESTIVE FIRS SWEATER

These samples show sizes XXS and 3X. Get everyone in the Christmas spirit with their own Festive Firs Sweater.

FILET CROCHET FACTS

As you've got this far in the book, I'll assume that you already have a budding interest in filet crochet. Congratulations, we're now best friends.

Filet crochet uses a combination of blocks of stitches and open mesh to create patterns, and traditionally you might associate it with doilies, or baby blankets. Did your nan have a long table runner with blocks of stitches creating floral shapes within a mesh-like base? That was most likely filet crochet. I have great memories of some 70s tablecloths passed down to my mum, and the skill they took to create was of a level I can only aspire to! However, the patterns within this book have an entirely different feel to the filet of years gone by, bringing it up to date and giving it a 21st century make-over. We're showing appreciation to our crafting ancestors by taking the methods they honed and tweaking them to fit our changing lifestyles.

The good news is that although it may not look it at first glance, filet crochet happens to be extremely straightforward. You're simply using chain spaces within the fabric of your crochet to create patterns, motifs and fun details. Most of the patterns in this book are suitable for a confident beginner. If you can double crochet (UK treble) and make a chain, you're all set for something as eye-catching as the Time After Time Sweater or the Cotton Candy Cardigan. Once you've gained momentum, you can easily start adding some bobbles to create Echo Beach, or some shells for Ocean Drive. Then, when you're feeling on top of the world, tackle the colour changes in the Bobble & Chic Cardigan to really showcase your skills! Before you get started, here are a few things that you need to remember.

Working chains

Unless instructed otherwise, always work into the chains of the previous row, not into the chain space. Working into the chain itself means your stitches will stack up nicely above each other, rather than sitting unevenly within the space. When working chains, make sure to work them loosely. You don't want to make an entire row and then realise you can't get your hook through. If you have a lot of chains in one row that are not loose enough, you're likely to notice some puckering in your work. So always remember, the #1 rule of this book is work your chains LOOSELY.

Another important thing to keep in mind is that although turning chains do not count as a stitch throughout the book, filet chains within your work always do. Let's use Festive Firs as an example. If you're making a size M, you have 76 stitches in Row 1. When you start working your filet in Row 6, you work 'ch2, sk 2 sts' four times within that row. That means you have 68 stitches and 8 chains, giving a total of 76 stitches. Always treat your chains as stitches and either work into them or skip over them as instructed. Don't ignore them, it hurts their feelings and it'll mess up your work.

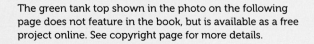

The green tank top shown in the photo on the following page does not feature in the book, but is available as a free project online. See copyright page for more details.

Charts

Traditionally a filet crochet chart would be made up of black and white squares, with white representing stitches and black representing chain spaces. However, because many of the makes in this book use a mix of stitches as well as filet, I've gone with charts that show the type of stitches alongside the chains.

Don't worry if you're not a fan of charts; they are simply there to show you where the chains and stitches in the filet pattern should be sitting in relation to each other, so you can easily see if you make any mistakes in the pattern repeats. There is no need to follow the chart – always work from the written instructions for your chosen size instead.

Charts can be read in either direction, see Pattern Notes for the item you are making for instructions. The filet pattern repeat is shown in the written instructions between two *, but the charts will often show a few of the stitches on either side of the repeat – not all of them, however, because the total number of stitches in a row or round will vary from size to size.

CHART SHOWING ONE REPEAT OF A FILET PATTERN

Filet stitches

Additional stitches in a row or round; the number of these will vary according to the size being worked.

THE
PROJECTS

OCEAN DRIVE CARDIGAN

The bobbles, shells and waves of filet in this cardigan remind me of standing on a pebbly beach with my toes in the water! It's the perfect summer cover up for strolls along the promenade. Get yourself an ice cream and meet me at the penny pushers!

Gauge (tension)

16 sts x 9 rows = 10 x 10cm (4 x 4in) using 4mm (US size G/6) hook.

Yarn & hook

Paintbox Yarns Simply DK (100% acrylic), DK (light worsted) weight yarn, 276m (302yd) per 100g (3½oz) ball in the following shade:
• Cerulean Blue (74): 4½ (4½, 4¾, 5½) (5¾, 6¼, 6¾) (8, 8½, 9) balls
4mm (US size G/6) crochet hook

	XXS	XS	S	M	L	XL	2X	3X	4X	5X
Circumference	85cm (33½in)	92.5cm (36½in)	100cm (39¼in)	110cm (43½in)	122.5cm (48¼in)	130cm (51¼in)	140cm (55in)	150cm (59in)	160cm (63in)	167.5cm (66in)
Length	50cm (19¾in)	50cm (19¾in)	50cm (19¾in)	59cm (23¼in)	59cm (23¼in)	59cm (23¼in)	59cm (23¼in)	68cm (26¾in)	68cm (26¾in)	68cm (26¾in)
Sleeve depth	19.5cm (7¾in)	19.5cm (7¾in)	19.5cm (7¾in)	19.5cm (7¾in)	21cm (8¼in)	21cm (8¼in)	21cm (8¼in)	25cm (9¾in)	27.5cm (10¾in)	27.5cm (10¾in)

Pattern notes & chart

The length of this cardigan is completely customisable – just work fewer or extra repeats, ending on a double crochet row. Note that if you make it longer, you may need more yarn.

Chart shows pattern repeat for guidance on stitch placement within the filet section only, place repeats within rows or rounds following written instructions for your chosen size. Read RS (even-number) rows from right to left and WS (odd-number) rows from left to right.

Special abbreviation

Bobble: [yo, insert hook into st, yo, pull through st, yo, pull through 2 loops on hook] 4 times, yo, pull through all remaining loops on hook

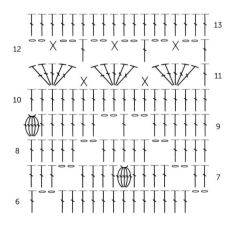

Back Panel

Row 1: Fdc68 (74, 80, 88) (98, 104, 112) (120, 128, 134), turn.

OR: Ch71 (77, 83, 91) (101, 107, 115) (123, 131, 137), 1dc in fourth ch from hook and each ch along, turn.

Row 2: Ch3 (does not count as a st throughout), [1FPdc, 1BPdc] to end, turn.

Rows 3 and 4: Rep row 2.

Row 5: Ch3, 1dc in each st, turn.

Sizes (XS, S) (L, 2X) (4X, 5X) only:

Row 6 (RS): Ch3, (4, 7) (7, 5) (4, 7) dc, *ch2, sk 2 sts, 13dc, ch2, sk 2 sts, 1dc* to last (1, 4) (4, 2) (1, 4) sts, 1dc in each rem st, turn.

Row 7 (WS): Ch3, (3, 6) (6, 4) (3, 6)dc, *ch2, sk 2 sts, 4dc, bobble, 4dc, ch 2, sk 2 sts, 5dc* to last (16, 19) (19, 17) (16, 19) sts, ch2, sk 2 sts, 4dc, bobble, 4dc, ch2, sk 2 sts, (3, 6) (6, 4) (3, 6)dc, turn.

Row 8: Ch3, (5, 8) (8, 6) (5, 8)dc, *ch2, sk 2 sts, 5dc, ch2, sk 2 sts, 9dc* to last (15, 18) (18, 16) (15, 18) sts, ch2, sk 2 sts, 5dc, ch2, sk 2 sts, (6, 9) (9, 7) (6, 9)dc, turn.

Sizes (XS) (4X) only:

Row 9: Ch3, (2) (2)dc, *6dc, ch2, sk 2 sts, 1dc, ch2, sk 2 sts, 6dc, bobble* to end, turn.

Sizes (S) (L, 2X) (5X) only:

Row 9: Ch3, (4) (4, 2) (4)dc, bobble, *6dc, ch2, sk 2 sts, 1dc, ch2, sk 2 sts, 6dc, bobble* to last (3) (3, 1) (3) sts, 1dc in each rem st, turn.

Sizes (XS, S) (L, 2X) (4X, 5X) only:

Row 10: Ch3, 1dc in each st, turn.

Row 11: Ch3, (1, 1) (1, 2) (1, 1) dc, *sk 2 sts, 5dc in next st, sk 2 sts, 1sc* to last (1, 1) (1, 2) (1, 1) sts, 1dc in each rem st, turn.

Row 12: Ch3, (2, 2) (2, 3) (2, 2) dc, *ch2, sk 2 sts, 1sc, ch2, sk 2 sts, 1dc* to last (6, 6) (6, 7) (6, 6) sts, ch2, sk 2 sts, 1sc, ch2, sk 2 sts, (1, 1) (1, 2) (1, 1)dc, turn.

NOTE: The Row 12 dc should sit in the Row 11 sc and the Row 12 sc in the centre dc of the Row 11 5-dc group.

Row 13: Ch3, 1dc in each st, turn.

Rep Rows 6–13 (4, 4) (5, 5) (6, 6) MORE times for a total of (45, 45) (53, 53) (61, 61) rows.

Sizes XXS (M) (XL) (3X) only:

Row 6 (RS): Ch3, 4 (5) (4) (3)dc, ch2, sk 2 sts, 1dc, *ch2, sk 2 sts, 13dc, ch2, sk 2 sts, 1dc* to last 7 (8) (7) (6) sts, ch2, sk 2 sts, 5 (6) (5) (4)dc, turn.

Row 7 (WS): Ch3, 3 (4) (3) (2)dc, ch2, sk 2 sts, 5dc, *ch2, sk 2 sts, 4dc, bobble, 4dc, ch2, sk 2 sts, 5dc* to last 4 (5) (4) (3) sts, ch2, sk 2 sts, 2 (3) (2) (1)dc, turn.

Row 8: Ch3, 11 (12) (11) (10) dc, *ch2, sk 2 sts, 5dc, ch2, sk 2 sts, 9dc* to last 3 (4) (3) (2) sts, 1dc in each rem st, turn.

Row 9: Ch3, 7 (8) (7) (6)dc, bobble, *6dc, ch2, sk 2 sts, 1dc, ch2, sk 2 sts, 6dc, bobble* to last 6 (7) (6) (5) sts, 1dc in each rem st, turn.

Row 10: Ch3, 1dc in each st, turn.

Row 11: Ch3, 1 (2) (1) (3)dc, *sk 2 sts, 5dc in next st, sk 2 sts, 1sc* to last 1 (2) (1) (3) sts, 1dc in each rem st, turn.

Row 12: Ch3, 2 (3) (2) (4)dc, *ch2, sk 2 sts, 1sc, ch2, sk 2 sts, 1dc* to last 6 (7) (6) (8) sts, ch2, sk 2 sts, 1sc, ch2, sk 2 sts, 1dc in each rem st, turn.

NOTE: The Row 12 dc should sit in the Row 11 sc and the Row 12 sc in the centre dc of the Row 11 5-dc group.

Row 13: Ch3, 1dc in each st, turn.

Rep Rows 6–13 four (five) (five) (six) MORE times for a total of 45 (53) (53) (61) rows.

Fasten off.

Front Panels
(make two)

Row 1: Fdc32 (32, 34, 38) (40, 44, 50) (52, 56, 60).

OR: Ch35 (35, 37, 41) (43, 47, 53) (55, 59, 63), 1dc in fourth ch from hook and each ch along, turn.

Row 2: Ch3 (does not count as a st throughout), [1FPdc, 1BPdc] to end, turn.

Rows 3 and 4: Rep Row 2.

Row 5: Ch3, 1dc in each st, turn.

Sizes XXS (XS, S) (2X) (3X) only:

Row 6 (RS): Ch3, 4 (4, 5) (4) (5) dc, ch2, sk 2 sts, 1dc, *ch2, sk 2 sts, 13dc, ch2, sk 2 sts, 1dc* to last 7 (7, 8) (7) (8) sts, ch2, sk 2 sts, 5 (5, 6) (5) (6)dc, turn.

Row 7 (WS): Ch3, 3 (3, 4) (3) (4)dc, *ch2, sk 2 sts, 5dc, ch2, sk 2 sts, 4dc, bobble, 4dc* to last 11 (11, 12) (11) (12) sts, ch2, sk 2 sts, 5dc, ch2, sk 2 sts, 2 (2, 3) (2) (3)dc, turn.

Sizes (S) (3X) only:

Row 8: Ch3, 1dc, ch2, sk 2 sts, (9) (9)dc, *ch2, sk 2 sts, 5dc, ch2, sk 2 sts, 9dc* to last (4) (4) sts, ch2, sk 2 sts, 1dc in each rem st, turn.

Sizes XXS (XS) (2X) only:

Row 8: Ch3, 11 (11) (11)dc, *ch2, sk 2 sts, 5dc, ch2, sk 2 sts, 9dc* to last 3 (3) (3) sts, 1dc in each rem st, turn.

Sizes XXS (XS, S) (2X) (3X) only:

Row 9: Ch3, 7 (7, 8) (7) (8)dc, bobble, *6dc, ch2, sk 2 sts, 1dc, ch2, sk 2 sts, 6dc, bobble* to last 6 (6, 7) (6) (7) sts, 1dc in each rem st, turn.

Row 10: Ch3, 1dc in each st, turn.

Row 11: Ch3, 1 (1, 2) (1) (2) dc, *sk 2 sts, 5dc in next st, sk 2 sts, 1sc* to last 1 (1, 2) (1) (2) sts, 1dc in each rem st, turn.

Row 12: Ch3, 2 (2, 3) (2) (2)dc, *ch2, sk 2 sts, 1sc, ch2, sk 2 sts, 1dc* to last 6 (6, 7) (6) (7) sts, ch2, sk 2 sts, 1sc, ch2, sk 2 sts, 1 (1, 2) (1) (2)dc, turn.

Row 13: Ch3, 1dc in each st, turn.

Rep Rows 6–13 until Front Panel is same length as Back Panel.

Seaming row: Ch1, with RS of Back and one Front Panel tog, 1sc through next 32 (32, 34) (50) (52) sts on both edges to seam shoulder.

Fasten off.

Rep Seaming Row with second Front Panel.

Sizes (M) (L, XL) (4X, 5X) only:

Row 6 (RS): Ch3, (1) (2, 4) (1, 3) dc, *ch2, sk 2 sts, 13dc, ch2, sk 2 sts, 1dc* to last (1) (2, 4) (1, 3) st, 1dc in each rem st, turn.

Row 7 (WS): Ch3, (4) (5, 7) (4, 6) dc, *ch2, sk 2 sts, 4dc, bobble, 4dc, ch2, sk 2 sts, 5dc* to last (16) (17, 19) (16, 18) sts, ch 2, sk 2 sts, 4dc, bobble, 4dc, ch2, sk 2 sts, (3) (4, 6) (3, 5)dc, turn.

Row 8: Ch3, (5) (6, 8) (5, 7)dc, *ch2, sk 2 sts, 5dc, ch2, sk 2 sts, 9dc* to last (15) (16, 18) (15, 17) sts, ch2, sk 2 sts, 5dc, ch2, sk 2 sts, (6) (7, 9) (6, 8)dc, turn.

Sizes (L, XL) (5X) only:

Row 9: Ch3, (2, 4) (3)dc, bobble, *6dc, ch2, sk 2 sts, 1dc, ch2, sk 2 sts, 6dc, bobble* to last (1, 3) (2) sts, 1dc in each rem st, turn.

Sizes (M) (4X) only:

Row 9: Ch3, (1) (1)dc, bobble, *6dc, ch2, sk 2 sts, 1dc, ch2, sk 2 sts, 6dc, bobble*, working 1dc in final st instead of bobble on last rep.

Sizes (M) (L, XL) (4X, 5X) only:

Row 10: Ch3, 1dc in each st, turn.

Row 11: Ch3, (1) (2, 1) (1, 3) dc, *sk 2 sts, 5dc in next st, sk 2 sts, 1sc* to last (1) (2, 1) (1, 3) sts, 1dc in each rem st, turn.

Row 12: Ch3, (2) (3, 2) (2, 4)dc, *ch2, sk 2 sts, 1sc, ch2, sk 2 sts, 1dc* to last (6) (7, 6) (6, 8) sts, ch2, sk 2 sts, 1sc, ch2, sk 2 sts, (1) (2, 1) (1, 3)dc, turn.

Row 13: Ch3, 1dc in each st, turn.

Rep Rows 6–13 until Front Panel is same length as Back Panel.

Seaming row: Ch1, with RS of Back and one Front Panel tog, 1sc through next (38) (40, 44) (56, 60) sts on both edges to seam shoulder.

Fasten off.

Rep Seaming Row with second Front Panel.

Sleeves
(make two)

Round 1: Ch31 (31, 31, 31) (34, 34, 34) (34, 36, 36), ss to join into a ring.

Round 2: Ch3 (does not count as a st throughout), 1dc in each st, ss to join, do not turn.

Sizes XXS (XS, S, M) only:

Round 3: Ch3, [1FPdc, 1BPdc] to last st, 1FPdc, ss to join, do not turn.

Rounds 4 and 5: Rep Round 2.

Sizes (L, XL, 2X) (3X, 4X, 5X) only:

Round 3: Ch3, [1FPdc, 1BPdc] to end, ss to join, do not turn.

Rounds 4 and 5: Rep Round 2.

Sizes XXS (XS, S, M) (L, XL, 2X) only:

Round 6: Ch3, 2dc in each st around, ss to join, do not turn. 62 (62, 62, 62) (68, 68, 68) sts

Sizes (3X, 4X, 5X) only:

Round 6: Ch3, 2dc in each of next (11, 10, 10) sts, 3dc in each of next (6, 8, 8) sts, 2dc in each of next (11, 10, 10) sts, 3dc in each of next (6, 8, 8) sts, ss to join, do not turn. (80, 88, 88) sts

All sizes:

Round 7 (RS): Ch3, 4 (4, 4, 4) (7, 7, 7) (4, 8, 8)dc, *ch2, sk 2 sts, 13dc, ch2, sk 2 sts, 1dc* to last 4 (4, 4, 4) (7, 7, 7) (4, 8, 8) sts, 1dc in each rem st, ss to join, turn.

Round 8 (WS): Ch3, 7 (7, 7, 7) (10, 10, 10) (7, 11, 11)dc, *ch2, sk 2 sts, 4dc, bobble, 4dc, ch2, sk 2 sts, 5dc* to last 1 (1, 1, 1) (4, 4, 4) (1, 5, 5) sts, 1dc in each rem st, ss to join, turn.

Round 9: Ch3, 8 (8, 8, 8) (11, 11, 11) (8, 12, 12)dc, *ch2, sk 2 sts, 5dc, ch2, sk 2 sts, 9dc* to last 0 (0, 0, 0) (3, 3, 3) (0, 4, 4) sts, 1dc in each rem st, ss to join, turn.

Round 10: Ch3, 4 (4, 4, 4) (7, 7, 7) (4, 8, 8)dc, bobble *6dc, ch2, sk 2 sts, 1dc, ch2, sk 2 sts, 6dc, bobble* to last 3 (3, 3, 3) (6, 6, 6) (3, 7, 7) sts, 1dc in each rem st, ss to join, turn.

Round 11: Ch3, 1dc in each st, ss to join, turn.

Round 12: Ch3, 0 (0, 0, 0) (0, 0, 0) (0, 1, 1)dc, *sk 2 sts, 5dc in next st, sk 2 sts, 1sc* to last 2 (2, 2, 2) (2, 2, 2) (2, 3, 3) sts, 1dc in each rem st, ss to join, turn.

Round 13: Ch3, 3 (3, 3, 3) (3, 3, 3) (3, 4, 4)dc, *ch2, sk 2 sts, 1sc, ch2, sk 2 sts, 1dc* to last 5 (5, 5, 5) (5, 5, 5) (5, 6, 6) sts, ch2, sk 2 sts, 1sc, ch2, sk 2 sts, 0 (0, 0, 0) (0, 0, 0) (0, 1, 1)dc, ss to join, turn.

Round 14: Ch3, 1dc in each st and ch, ss to join, turn.

Rep Rounds 7–14 four more times for a total of 46 rounds.

Fasten off.

Finishing

Seam sides and join Sleeves to body panels.

Edging

With RS facing, join yarn at bottom hem on left Front Panel.

Row 1: Ch1, 2sc in each row end along left Front Panel, 1sc in each st along back of neckline, 2sc in each row end on right Front Panel, turn.

Row 2: Ch1, 1sc in each st.

Fasten off and weave in all ends.

TIME AFTER TIME SWEATER

Easily one of my most popular patterns, the Time After Time Sweater has had a revamp and is now better than ever! It is worked here in a DK (light worsted) weight yarn, but you could also work it in an aran (worsted) weight yarn with the same heart motif (see Pattern Notes for more details).

Gauge (tension)

16 sts x 9 rows = 10 x 10cm (4 x 4in) using 4mm (US size G/6) hook.

Yarn & hook

Paintbox Yarns Simply DK (100% acrylic), DK (light worsted) weight yarn, 276m (302yd) per 100g (3½oz) ball in the following shade:
• Dusty Rose (141): 4 (4¼, 4¾, 5) (6, 6¼, 7) (7¾, 8½, 8¾) balls

4mm (US size G/6) crochet hook

	XXS	XS	S	M	L	XL	2X	3X	4X	5X
Circumference	82.5cm (32½in)	90cm (35½in)	102.5cm (40¼in)	110cm (43½in)	122.5cm (48¼in)	130cm (51¼in)	142.5cm (56in)	150cm (59in)	162.5cm (64in)	170cm (67in)
Length	51cm (20in)	51cm (20in)	51cm (20in)	51cm (20in)	59cm (23¼in)	59cm (23¼in)	59cm (23¼in)	66.5cm (26¼in)	66.5cm (26¼in)	66.5cm (26¼in)
Sleeve depth	16cm (6¼in)	17cm (6¾in)	18cm (7in)	19cm (7½in)	20.5cm (8in)	22cm (8¾in)	24cm (9½in)	24cm (9½in)	25.5cm (10in)	26cm (10¼in)

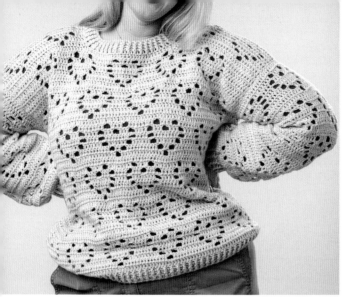

Pattern notes & chart

To make this sweater in aran (worsted) yarn, follow the Festive Firs Sweater pattern, but work the heart repeats between the two * from this pattern. Make sure to work the repeats in full because there are stitches before and after the filet. For example, Row 5 is *7dc, ch2, sk 2 sts, 7dc*, NOT *7dc, ch2, sk 2 sts*. If you forget those 7dc at the end of each repeat, the rest of the pattern won't work.

Chart shows pattern repeat for guidance on stitch placement within the filet section only, place repeats within rows or rounds following written instructions for your chosen size. Read RS (odd-number) rows from right to left and WS (even-number) rows from left to right.

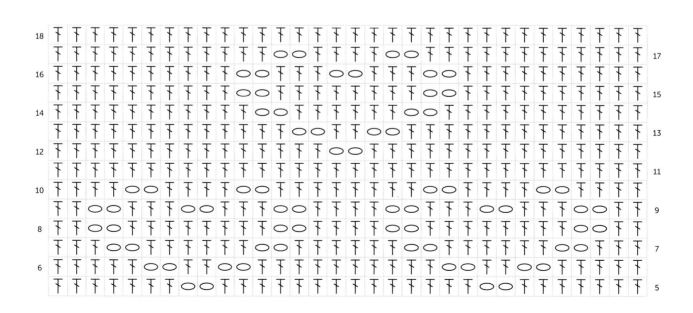

Back Panel

Row 1: Fdc66 (72, 82, 88) (98, 104, 114) (120, 130, 136), turn.

OR: Ch69 (75, 85, 91) (101, 107, 117) (123, 133, 139), 1dc in fourth ch from hook and each ch along, turn.

Row 2: Ch3 (does not count as a st throughout), [1FPdc, 1BPdc] to end, turn.

Rows 3 and 4: Rep Row 2.

Heart section one

Row 5 (RS): Ch3, 1 (4, 1, 4) (1, 4, 1) (4, 1, 4)dc, *7dc, ch2, sk 2 sts, 7dc* 4 (4, 5, 5) (6, 6, 7) (7, 8, 8) times, 1 (4, 1, 4) (1, 4, 1) (4, 1, 4)dc, turn.

Row 6 (WS): Ch3, 1 (4, 1, 4) (1, 4, 1) (4, 1, 4)dc, *5dc, ch2, sk 2 sts, 2dc, ch2, sk 2 sts, 5dc* 4 (4, 5, 5) (6, 6, 7) (7, 8, 8) times, 1 (4, 1, 4) (1, 4, 1) (4, 1, 4)dc, turn.

Row 7: Ch3, 1 (4, 1, 4) (1, 4, 1) (4, 1, 4)dc, *3dc, ch2, sk 2 sts, 6dc, ch2, sk 2 sts, 3dc* 4 (4, 5, 5) (6, 6, 7) (7, 8, 8) times, 1 (4, 1, 4) (1, 4, 1) (4, 1, 4)dc, turn.

Row 8: Ch3, 1 (4, 1, 4) (1, 4, 1) (4, 1, 4)dc, *2dc, ch2, sk 2 sts, 8dc, ch2, sk 2 sts, 2dc* 4 (4, 5, 5) (6, 6, 7) (7, 8, 8) times, 1 (4, 1, 4) (1, 4, 1) (4, 1, 4)dc, turn.

Row 9: Ch3, 1 (4, 1, 4) (1, 4, 1) (4, 1, 4)dc, *2dc, ch2, sk 2 sts, 3dc, ch2, sk 2 sts, 3dc, ch2, sk 2 sts, 2dc* 4 (4, 5, 5) (6, 6, 7) (7, 8, 8) times, 1 (4, 1, 4) (1, 4, 1) (4, 1, 4)dc, turn.

Row 10: Ch3, 1 (4, 1, 4) (1, 4, 1) (4, 1, 4)dc, *4dc, ch2, sk 2 sts, 4dc, ch2, sk 2 sts, 4dc* 4 (4, 5, 5) (6, 6, 7) (7, 8, 8) times, 1 (4, 1, 4) (1, 4, 1) (4, 1, 4)dc, turn.

Row 11: Ch3, 1dc in each st, turn.

Heart section two

Row 12: Ch3, 9 (12, 9, 12) (9, 12, 9) (12, 9, 12)dc, *7dc, ch2, sk 2 sts, 7dc* 3 (3, 4, 4) (5, 5, 6) (6, 7, 7) times, 9 (12, 9, 12) (9, 12, 9) (12, 9, 12)dc, turn.

Row 13: Ch3, 9 (12, 9, 12) (9, 12, 9) (12, 9, 12)dc, *5dc, ch2, sk 2 sts, 2dc, ch2, sk 2 sts, 5dc* 3 (3, 4, 4) (5, 5, 6) (6, 7, 7) times, 9 (12, 9, 12) (9, 12, 9) (12, 9, 12)dc, turn.

Row 14: Ch3, 9 (12, 9, 12) (9, 12, 9) (12, 9, 12)dc, *3dc, ch2, sk 2 sts, 6dc, ch2, sk 2 sts, 3dc* 3 (3, 4, 4) (5, 5, 6) (6, 7, 7) times, 9 (12, 9, 12) (9, 12, 9) (12, 9, 12)dc, turn.

Row 15: Ch3, 9 (12, 9, 12) (9, 12, 9) (12, 9, 12)dc, *2dc, ch2, sk 2 sts, 8dc, ch2, sk 2 sts, 2dc* 3 (3, 4, 4) (5, 5, 6) (6, 7, 7) times, 9 (12, 9, 12) (9, 12, 9) (12, 9, 12)dc, turn.

Row 16: Ch3, 9 (12, 9, 12) (9, 12, 9) (12, 9, 12)dc, *2dc, ch2, sk 2 sts, 3dc, ch2, sk 2 sts, 3dc, ch2, sk 2 sts, 2dc* 3 (3, 4, 4) (5, 5, 6) (6, 7, 7) times, 9 (12, 9, 12) (9, 12, 9) (12, 9, 12)dc, turn.

Row 17: Ch3, 9 (12, 9, 12) (9, 12, 9) (12, 9, 12)dc, *4dc, ch2, sk 2 sts, 4dc, ch2, sk 2 sts, 4dc* 3 (3, 4, 4) (5, 5, 6) (6, 7, 7) times, 9 (12, 9, 12) (9, 12, 9) (12, 9, 12)dc, turn.

Row 18: Ch3, 1dc in each st, turn.

Rep Heart Sections One and Two 2 (2, 2, 2) (2, 2, 2) (3, 3, 3) MORE times.

Sizes (L, XL, 2X) only:

Rep Heart Section One once more.

All sizes:

There is now a total of 46 (46, 46, 46) (53, 53, 53) (60, 60, 60) rows.

Fasten off.

> TIP: You can alter the length of your sweater by working additional or fewer repeats. Remove them from the bottom rather than the top, to avoid neckline issues. For example, for one less repeat, start with Heart Section Two.

Front Panel

Work as per Back Panel until one Heart Section short of finished length, then work Neckline One.

Neckline one

Sizes XXS (XS) only:

Row 1: Ch3, 19 (22)dc, turn.

Row 2: Ch3, 1dc in each st, turn.

Rows 3–7: Rep Row 2.

Row 8: Ch1, with RS of Front and Back Panels tog, 1sc through next 19 (22) sts on both edges to seam shoulder.

Fasten off.

Move to Neckline Two.

Sizes (S, M) (3X, 4X, 5X) only:

Row 1: Ch3, (9, 12) (12, 9, 12)dc, *7dc, ch2, sk 2 sts, 7dc* (1, 1) (1, 2, 2) times, (1, 1) (14, 6, 6)dc, turn.

Row 2: Ch3, (1, 1) (14, 6, 6)dc, *5dc, ch2, sk 2 sts, 2dc, ch2, sk 2 sts, 5dc* (1, 1) (1, 2, 2) times, (9, 12) (12, 9, 12)dc, turn.

Row 3: Ch3, (9, 12) (12, 9, 12) dc, *3dc, ch2, sk 2 sts, 6dc, ch2, sk 2 sts, 3dc* (1, 1) (1, 2, 2) times, (1, 1) (14, 6, 6)dc, turn.

Row 4: Ch3, (1, 1) (14, 6, 6)dc, *2dc, ch2, sk 2 sts, 8dc, ch2, sk 2 sts, 2dc* (1, 1) (1, 2, 2) times, (9, 12) (12, 9, 12)dc, turn.

Row 5: Ch3, (9, 12) (12, 9, 12)dc, *2dc, ch2, sk 2 sts, 3dc, ch2, sk 2 sts, 3dc, ch2, sk 2 sts, 2dc* (1, 1) (1, 2, 2) times, (1, 1) (14, 6, 6)dc, turn.

Row 6: Ch3, (1, 1) (14, 6, 6)dc, *4dc, ch2, sk 2 sts, 4dc, ch2, sk 2 sts, 4dc* (1, 1) (1, 2, 2) times, (9, 12) (12, 9, 12)dc, turn.

Row 7: Ch3, 1dc in each st, turn.

Row 8: Ch1, with RS of Front and Back Panels tog, 1sc through next (26, 29) (42, 47, 50) sts on both edges to seam shoulder.

Fasten off.

Move to Neckline Two.

Sizes (L, XL, 2X) only:

Row 1: Ch3, (1, 4, 1)dc, *7dc, ch2, sk 2 sts, 7dc* twice, (1, 0, 7)dc, turn.

Row 2: Ch3, (1, 0, 7)dc, *5dc, ch2, sk 2 sts, 2dc, ch2, sk 2 sts, 5dc* twice, (1, 4, 1)dc, turn.

Row 3: Ch3, (1, 4, 1) dc, *3dc, ch2, sk 2 sts, 6dc, ch2, sk 2 sts, 3dc* twice, (1, 0, 7)dc, turn.

Row 4: Ch3, (1, 0, 7)dc, *2dc, ch2, sk 2 sts, 8dc, ch2, sk 2 sts, 2dc* twice, (1, 4, 1)dc, turn.

Row 5: Ch3, (1, 4, 1)dc, *2dc, ch2, sk 2 sts, 3dc, ch2, sk 2 sts, 3dc, ch2, sk 2 sts, 2dc* twice, (1, 0, 7) dc, turn.

Row 6: Ch3, (1, 0, 7)dc, *4dc, ch2, sk 2 sts, 4dc, ch2, sk 2 sts, 4dc* twice, (1, 4, 1)dc, turn.

Row 7: Ch3, 1dc in each st, turn.

Row 8: Ch1, with RS of Front and Back Panels tog, 1sc through next (32, 36, 40) sts on both edges to seam shoulder.

Fasten off.

Neckline two

Count 19 (22, 26, 29) (32, 36, 40) (42, 47, 50) sts from other edge of work and join yarn.

Sizes XXS (XS) only:

Row 1: Ch3, 19 (22)dc, turn.

Row 2: Ch3, 1dc in each st, turn.

Rows 3–7: Rep Row 2.

Row 8: Ch1, with RS of Front and Back Panels tog, 1sc through next 19 (22) sts on both edges to seam shoulder.

Fasten off.

Sizes (S, M) (3X, 4X, 5X) only:

Row 1: Ch3, (1, 1) (14, 6, 6)dc, *7dc, ch2, sk 2 sts, 7dc* (1, 1) (1, 2, 2) times, (9, 12) (12, 9, 12)dc, turn.

Row 2: Ch3, (9, 12) (12, 9, 12) dc, *5dc, ch2, sk 2 sts, 2dc, ch2, sk 2 sts, 5dc* (1, 1) (1, 2, 2) times, (1, 1) (14, 6, 6)dc, turn.

Row 3: Ch3, (1, 1) (14, 6, 6)dc, *3dc, ch2, sk 2 sts, 6dc, ch2, sk 2 sts, 3dc* (1, 1) (1, 2, 2) times, (9, 12) (12, 9, 12)dc, turn.

Row 4: Ch3, (9, 12) (12, 9, 12) dc, *2dc, ch2, sk 2 sts, 8dc, ch2, sk 2 sts, 2dc* (1, 1) (1, 2, 2) times, (1, 1) (14, 6, 6)dc, turn.

Row 5: Ch3, (1, 1) (14, 6, 6)dc, *2dc, ch2, sk 2 sts, 3dc, ch2, sk 2 sts, 3dc, ch2, sk 2 sts, 2dc* (1, 1) (1, 2, 2) times, (9, 12) (12, 9, 12)dc, turn.

Row 6: Ch3, (9, 12) (12, 9, 12) dc, *4dc, ch2, sk 2 sts, 4dc, ch2, sk 2 sts, 4dc* (1, 1) (1, 2, 2) times, (1, 1) (14, 6, 6)dc, turn.

Row 7: Ch3, 1dc in each st, turn.

Row 8: Ch1, with RS of Front and Back Panels tog, 1sc through next (26, 29) (42, 47, 50) sts on both edges to seam shoulder.

Fasten off.

Sizes (L, XL, 2X) only:

Row 1: Ch3, (1, 0, 7)dc, *7dc, ch2, sk 2 sts, 7dc* twice, (1, 4, 1)dc, turn.

Row 2: Ch3, (1, 4, 1)dc, *5dc, ch2, sk 2 sts, 2dc, ch2, sk 2 sts, 5dc* twice, (1, 0, 7)dc, turn.

Row 3: Ch3, (1, 0, 7)dc, *3dc, ch2, sk 2 sts, 6dc, ch2, sk 2 sts, 3dc* twice, (1, 4, 1)dc, turn.

Row 4: Ch3, (1, 4, 1)dc, *2dc, ch2, sk 2 sts, 8dc, ch2, sk 2 sts, 2dc* twice, (1, 0, 7)dc, turn.

Row 5: Ch3, (1, 0, 7)dc, *2dc, ch2, sk 2 sts, 3dc, ch2, sk 2 sts, 3dc, ch2, sk 2 sts, 2dc* twice, (1, 4, 1)dc, turn.

Row 6: Ch3, (1, 4, 1)dc, *4dc, ch2, sk 2 sts, 4dc, ch2, sk 2 sts, 4dc* twice, (1, 0, 7)dc, turn.

Row 7: Ch3, 1dc in each st, turn.

Row 8: Ch1, with RS of Front and Back Panels tog, 1sc through next (32, 36, 40) sts on both edges to seam shoulder.

Fasten off.

Sleeves

(make two)

Round 1: Ch30 (30, 30, 30) (32, 32, 34) (34, 34, 34), ss to join into a ring.

Round 2 (RS): Ch3 (does not count as a st throughout), 1dc in each st, ss to join, do not turn.

Round 3: Ch3, [1FPdc, 1BPdc] to end, ss to join, do not turn.

Rounds 4 and 5: Rep Round 3.

Sizes XXS (XS, S) only

Round 6: Ch3, 1dc in each of next 4 (3, 1) sts, 2dc in each of next 22 (24, 28) sts, 1dc in each of next 4 (3, 1) sts, ss to join, turn. 52 (54, 58) sts

Size (M) only

Round 6: Ch3, 2dc in each st, ss to join, turn. (60) sts

Sizes (L, XL, 2X) (3X, 4X, 5X) only:

Round 6: Ch3, 3dc in each of next (1, 3, 4) (4, 7, 8) sts, 2dc in each of next (15, 13, 13) (13, 10, 9) sts, 3dc in each of next (1, 3, 4) (4, 7, 8) sts, 2dc in each of next (15, 13, 13) (13, 10, 9) sts, ss to join, turn. (66, 70, 76) (76, 82, 84) sts

All sizes:

Heart section one

Round 7: Ch3, 2 (3, 5, 6) (1, 3, 6) (6, 1, 2)dc, *7dc, ch2, sk 2 sts, 7dc* 3 (3, 3, 3) (4, 4, 4) (4, 5, 5) times, 2 (3, 5, 6) (1, 3, 6) (6, 1, 2)dc, ss to join, turn.

Round 8: Ch3, 2 (3, 5, 6) (1, 3, 6) (6, 1, 2)dc, *5dc, ch2, sk 2 sts, 2dc, ch2, sk 2 sts, 5dc* 3 (3, 3, 3) (4, 4, 4) (4, 5, 5) times, 2 (3, 5, 6) (1, 3, 6) (6, 1, 2)dc, ss to join, turn.

Round 9: Ch3, 2 (3, 5, 6) (1, 3, 6) (6, 1, 2)dc, *3dc, ch2, sk 2 sts, 6dc, ch2, sk 2 sts, 3dc* 3 (3, 3, 3) (4, 4, 4) (4, 5, 5) times, 2 (3, 5, 6) (1, 3, 6) (6, 1, 2)dc, ss to join, turn.

Round 10: Ch3, 2 (3, 5, 6) (1, 3, 6) (6, 1, 2)dc, *2dc, ch2, sk 2 sts, 8dc, ch2, sk 2 sts, 2dc* 3 (3, 3, 3) (4, 4, 4) (4, 5, 5) times, 2 (3, 5, 6) (1, 3, 6) (6, 1, 2)dc, ss to join, turn.

Round 11: Ch3, 2 (3, 5, 6) (1, 3, 6) (6, 1, 2)dc, *2dc, ch2, sk 2 sts, 3dc, ch2, sk 2 sts, 3dc, ch2, sk 2 sts, 2dc* 3 (3, 3, 3) (4, 4, 4) (4, 5, 5) times, 2 (3, 5, 6) (1, 3, 6) (6, 1, 2)dc, ss to join, turn.

Round 12: Ch3, 2 (3, 5, 6) (1, 3, 6) (6, 1, 2)dc, *4dc, ch2, sk 2 sts, 4dc, ch2, sk 2 sts, 4dc* 3 (3, 3, 3) (4, 4, 4) (4, 5, 5) times, 2 (3, 5, 6) (1, 3, 6) (6, 1, 2)dc, ss to join, turn.

Round 13: Ch3, 1dc in each st, ss to join, turn.

Heart section two

Round 14: Ch3, 10 (11, 13, 14) (9, 11, 14) (14, 9, 10)dc, *7dc, ch2, sk 2 sts, 7dc* 2 (2, 2, 2) (3, 3, 3) (3, 4, 4) times, 10 (11, 13, 14) (9, 11, 14) (14, 9, 10)dc, ss to join, turn.

Round 15: Ch3, 10 (11, 13, 14) (9, 11, 14) (14, 9, 10)dc, *5dc, ch2, sk 2 sts, 2dc, ch2, sk 2 sts, 5dc* 2 (2, 2, 2) (3, 3, 3) (3, 4, 4) times, 10 (11, 13, 14) (9, 11, 14) (14, 9, 10)dc, ss to join, turn.

Round 16: Ch3, 10 (11, 13, 14) (9, 11, 14) (14, 9, 10)dc, *3dc, ch2, sk 2 sts, 6dc, ch2, sk 2 sts, 3dc* 2 (2, 2, 2) (3, 3, 3) (3, 4, 4) times, 10 (11, 13, 14) (9, 11, 14) (14, 9, 10)dc, ss to join, turn.

Round 17: Ch3, 10 (11, 13, 14) (9, 11, 14) (14, 9, 10)dc, *2dc, ch2, sk 2 sts, 8dc, ch2, sk 2 sts, 2dc* 2 (2, 2, 2) (3, 3, 3) (3, 4, 4) times, 10 (11, 13, 14) (9, 11, 14) (14, 9, 10)dc, ss to join, turn.

Round 18: Ch3, 10 (11, 13, 14) (9, 11, 14) (14, 9, 10)dc, *2dc, ch2, sk 2 sts, 3dc, ch2, sk 2 sts, 3dc, ch2, sk 2 sts, 2dc* 2 (2, 2, 2) (3, 3, 3) (3, 4, 4) times, 10 (11, 13, 14) (9, 11, 14) (14, 9, 10)dc, ss to join, turn.

Round 19: Ch3, 10 (11, 13, 14) (9, 11, 14) (14, 9, 10)dc, *4dc, ch2, sk 2 sts, 4dc, ch2, sk 2 sts, 4dc* 2 (2, 2, 2) (3, 3, 3) (3, 4, 4) times, 10 (11, 13, 14) (9, 11, 14) (14, 9, 10)dc, ss to join, turn.

Round 20: Ch3, 1dc in each st, ss to join, turn.

Rep Heart Sections One and Two once more, then rep Heart Section One a final time for a total of 41 rows.

Fasten off.

Finishing

Seam sides and join Sleeves to body panels.

Neckline edging

With RS facing, join yarn in any st at back of neckline.

Round 1: Ch3, 1dc in each st at back of neckline, 2dc in each Neckline One row end, 1dc in each st at front of neckline, 2dc in each Neckline Two row end, 1dc in each rem st at back of neckline, ss to join, do not turn.

Round 2: Ch3, [1FPdc, 1BPdc] to end, ss to join, do not turn.

Round 3: Rep Round 2.

Round 4: Rep Round 2.

Fasten off and weave in ends.

ECHO BEACH SWEATER

This is a personal favourite of mine and is easily one of my most worn pieces. The mix of stitches creates a great texture, and the repeats make it a really fun project to work on. Not so repetitive you get bored, but not so different every row that you need to pay too much attention. Pop a box set on and you'll have this one made in no time!

Gauge (tension)

16 sts x 9 rows = 10 x 10cm (4 x 4in) using 4mm (US size G/6) hook.

Yarn & hook

Paintbox Yarns Simply DK (100% acrylic), DK (light worsted) weight yarn, 276m (302yd) per 100g (3½oz) ball in the following shade:
• Dolphin Blue (136): 3¾ (4¼, 4½, 5) (5¼, 5¾, 6¾) (7, 8, 8¼) balls
4mm (US size G/6) crochet hook

	XXS	XS	S	M	L	XL	2X	3X	4X	5X
Circumference	81cm (32in)	89cm (35in)	96cm (37¾in)	107.5cm (42¼in)	122.5cm (48¼in)	130cm (51¼in)	145cm (57in)	152cm (59¾in)	164cm (64½in)	175cm (69in)
Length	52cm (20½in)	59cm (23¼in)	59cm (23¼in)	59cm (23¼in)	65.5cm (25¾in)	65.5cm (25¾in)	65.5cm (25¾in)	72cm (28¼in)	72cm (28¼in)	72cm (28¼in)
Sleeve depth	17.5cm (7in)	17.5cm (7in)	17.5cm (7in)	19cm (7½in)	19cm (7½in)	22cm (8¾in)	22cm (8¾in)	25cm (9¾in)	25cm (9¾in)	29.5cm (11½in)

Pattern notes & chart

As with many patterns in the book, you can easily adjust the length of your piece by working more or fewer repeats. Just be sure to end on a Row 11 repeat, and then work your final row. The panels are all worked flat from the bottom up and the sleeves are worked flat and seamed at the end.

Chart shows pattern repeat for guidance on stitch placement within the filet section only, place repeats within rows or rounds following written instructions for your chosen size. Read RS (odd-number) rows from right to left and WS (even-number) rows from left to right.

Special abbreviation

Bobble: [yo, insert hook into st, yo, pull through st, yo, pull through 2 loops on hook] 4 times, yo, pull through all remaining loops on hook

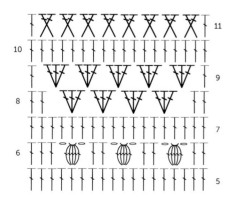

Back Panel

Row 1: Fdc65 (71, 77, 86) (98, 104, 116) (122, 131, 140), turn.

OR: Ch68 (74, 80, 89) (101, 107, 119) (125, 134, 143), 1dc in fourth ch from hook and each ch along, turn.

Sizes XXS (XS, S) (4X) only:

Row 2: Ch2 (does not count as a st throughout), [1FPdc, 1BPdc] to last st, 1FPdc, turn.

Row 3: Ch2, [1BPdc, 1FPdc] to last st, 1BPdc, turn.

Row 4: Rep Row 2.

Sizes (M) (L, XL, 2X) (3X, 5X) only:

Row 2: Ch2, [1FPdc, 1BPdc] to end, turn.

Rows 3 and 4: Rep Row 2.

All sizes:

Row 5 (RS): Ch3 (does not count as a st throughout), 1dc in each st, turn.

Row 6 (WS): Ch3, 3 (3, 4, 3) (2, 2, 3) (4, 3, 3)dc, *ch1, sk 1 st, bobble, ch1, sk 1 st, 2dc* to last 2 (3, 3, 3) (1, 2, 3) (3, 3, 2) sts, 1dc in each rem st, turn.

Row 7: Ch3, 1dc in each st, turn.

Row 8: Ch3, 2dc, *sk 2 sts, 3dc in next st* to last 3 sts, sk 2 sts, 2dc in final st, turn.

Row 9: Ch3, 1dc, 3dc in each sp between 3-dc groups from prev row, 1dc in final st, turn.

Row 10: Ch3, 1dc in each st, turn.

Row 11: Ch3, 1dc, *sk 1 st, 1dc in next st, 1dc in skipped st* to last 2 (2, 2, 1) (1, 1, 1) (1, 2, 1) st(s), 1dc in each rem st, turn.

Rep Rows 6–11 six (seven, seven, seven) (eight, eight, eight) (nine, nine, nine) MORE times for a total of 47 (53, 53, 53) (59, 59, 59) (65, 65, 65) rows.

Final row: Ch3, 1dc in each st.

Fasten off.

TIP: You can work less repeats for a cropped fit or add more if you need additional length. You must end on a Row 11 repeat, then work the Final Row.

Front Panel

Work as per Back Panel until 6 rows short of finished length, ending on a Row 6 rep, then work Neckline One.

Neckline one

Row 1: Ch3, 20 (23, 26, 29) (32, 35, 41) (44, 47, 53)dc, turn.

Row 2: Ch3, 2dc, *sk 2 sts, 3dc in the next st* to last 3 sts, sk 2 sts, 2dc in final st, turn.

Row 3: Ch3, 1dc, 3dc in each sp between 3-dc goups from prev row, 1dc in final st, turn.

Row 4: Ch3, 1dc in each st, turn.

Row 5: Ch3, 1dc, *sk 1 st, 1dc in next st, 1dc in skipped st* to last 1 (2, 1, 2) (1, 2, 2) (1, 2, 2) st(s), 1dc in each rem st, turn.

Row 6: Ch3, 1dc in each st, turn.

Row 7: Ch1, with RS of Front and Back Panels tog, 1sc through next 20 (23, 26, 29) (32, 35, 41) (44, 47, 53) sts on both edges to seam shoulder.

Fasten off.

Neckline two

Count 20 (23, 26, 29) (32, 35, 41) (44, 47, 53) sts from other edge of work and join yarn.

Row 1: Ch3, 20 (23, 26, 29) (32, 35, 41) (44, 47, 53)dc, turn.

Row 2: Ch3, 2dc, *sk 2 sts, 3dc in next st* to last 3 sts, sk 2 sts, 2dc in final st, turn.

Row 3: Ch3, 1dc, 3dc in each sp between 3-dc groups from prev row, 1dc in final st, turn.

Row 4: Ch3, 1dc in each st, turn.

Row 5: Ch3, 1 (2, 1, 2) (1, 2, 2) (1, 2, 2) dc, *sk 1 st, 1dc in next st, 1dc in skipped st* to last st, 1dc, turn.

Row 6: Ch3, 1dc in each st, turn.

Row 7: Ch1, with RS of Front and Back Panels tog, 1sc through next 20 (23, 26, 29) (32, 35, 41) (44, 47, 53) sts on both edges to seam shoulder.

Fasten off.

Sleeves
(make two)

NOTE: See sizing table for finished sleeve depths and work size that suits you best.

Row 1: Fdc29 (29, 29, 32) (32, 32, 32) (32, 38, 38), turn.

OR: Ch32 (32, 32, 35) (35, 35, 35) (35, 41, 41), 1dc in third ch from hook and each ch along, turn.

Sizes XXS (XS, S) only:

Row 2: Ch2 (does not count as a st throughout), [1FPdc, 1BPdc] to last st, 1FPdc, turn.

Row 3: Ch2, [1BPdc, 1FPdc] to last st, 1BPdc, turn.

Row 4: Rep Row 2.

Sizes (M) (L, XL, 2X) (3X, 4X, 5X) only:

Row 2: Ch2, [1FPdc, 1BPdc] to end, turn.

Rows 3 and 4: Rep Row 2.

Sizes XXS (XS, S) only:

Row 5: Ch3 (does not count as a st throughout), 2dc, 2dc in each rem st, turn. 56 (56, 56) sts

Sizes (M) (L) only:

Row 5: Ch3, 1dc, 2dc in each st to last st, 1dc, turn. (62) (62) sts

Sizes (XL, 2X) only:

Row 5: Ch3, 3dc in each of the first 3 sts, 2dc in each st to last 4 sts, 3dc in each rem st, turn. (71, 71) sts

Sizes (3X, 4X, 5X) only:

Row 5: Ch3, 3dc in each of first (8, 9, 9) sts, 2dc in each st to last 8 (10, 10) sts, 3dc in each rem st, turn. (80, 95, 95) sts

All sizes:

Row 6 (WS): Ch3, 3 (3, 3, 4) (4, 3, 3) (2, 4, 4)dc, *ch1, sk 1 st, bobble, ch1, sk 1 st, 2dc* to last 3 (3, 3, 3) (3, 3, 3) (3, 1, 1) sts, 1dc in each rem st, turn.

Row 7: Ch3, 1dc in each st, turn.

Row 8: Ch3, 2dc, *sk 2 sts, 3dc in next st* to last 3 sts, sk 2 sts, 2dc in final st, turn.

Row 9: Ch3, 1dc, 3dc in each sp between 3-dc groups from prev row, 1dc in final st, turn.

Row 10: Ch3, 1dc in each st, turn.

Row 11: Ch3, 1dc, *sk 1 st, 1dc in next st, 1dc in skipped st* to last 1 (1, 1, 1) (1, 2, 2) (1, 2, 2) st(s), 1dc in each rem st, turn.

Rep Rows 6–11 until Sleeve is desired length, approx. 40 (40, 42, 42) (42, 42, 42) (42, 42, 42) rows, ending on any row.

Final row: Ch3, 1dc in each st, turn.

Seaming row: Ch1, fold Sleeve in half lengthways with RS tog, 2dc through each row end on both sides to first row.

Fasten off.

Finishing

Seam sides and join Sleeves to body panels.

Neckline edging

Join yarn in any st at back of neckline.

Round 1: Ch3, 1dc in each st along back of neckline, 2dc in each row end from Neckline One, 1dc in each st along front of neckline, 2dc in each row end from Neckline Two, 1dc in each rem st, ss in ch-3 to join.

Round 2: Ch2, [1FPdc, 1BPdc] around, ss in ch-2 to join.

Round 3: Rep Round 2.

Round 4: Rep Round 2.

Fasten off and weave in all ends.

SILVER LININGS SWEATER

Look on the bright side with the Silver Linings Sweater. Enjoyable stitch repeats slowly fade to create a staggered chevron pattern over a summer-friendly sweater in a DK (light worsted) weight yarn. Perfect for testing the waters with some slightly more intricate filet once you've mastered the basic techniques.

Gauge (tension)

16 sts x 9 rows = 10 x 10cm (4 x 4in) using 4mm (US size G/6) hook.

Yarn & hook

Paintbox Yarns Simply DK (100% acrylic), DK (light worsted) weight yarn, 276m (302yd) per 100g (3½oz) ball in the following shade:
• Banana Cream (120): 3¼ (3¾, 4½, 4¾) (5½, 5¾, 6½) (7, 7½, 7¾) balls

4mm (US size G/6) crochet hook

	XXS	XS	S	M	L	XL	2X	3X	4X	5X
Circumference	85cm (33½in)	92.5cm (36½in)	105cm (41¼in)	112.5cm (44¼in)	125cm (49¼in)	132.5cm (52¼in)	145cm (57in)	152.5cm (60in)	165cm (65in)	172.5cm (68in)
Length	50cm (19¾in)	54cm (21¼in)	59cm (23¼in)	59cm (23¼in)	63cm (24¾in)	63cm (24¾in)	63cm (24¾in)	67.5cm (26½in)	67.5cm (26½in)	67.5cm (26½in)
Sleeve depth	16cm (6¼in)	17cm (6¾in)	17.5cm (7in)	19.5cm (7¾in)	21cm (8¼in)	21.5cm (8½in)	24cm (9½in)	25cm (9¾in)	26cm (10¼in)	26.5cm (10½in)

Pattern notes & chart

Chart shows pattern repeat for guidance on stitch placement within the filet section only and does not have row or stitch numbers because it shows different areas of pattern on one chart. Place repeats within rows or rounds following written instructions for your chosen size.

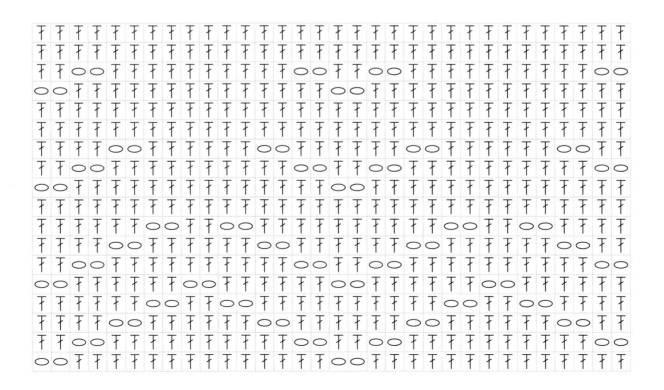

Back Panel

Row 1: Fdc68 (74, 84, 90) (100, 106, 116) (122, 132, 138), turn.

OR: Ch71 (77, 87, 93) (103, 109, 119) (125, 137, 141), 1dc in fourth ch from hook and each ch along, turn.

Sizes XXS (S) (L, 2X) (4X):

Row 2: Ch2 (does not count as a st throughout), [2FPdc, 2BPdc] to end, turn.

Rows 3 and 4: Rep Row 2.

Sizes (XS, M) (XL) (3X, 5X) only:

Row 2: Ch2, [2FPdc, 2BPdc] to last 2 sts, 2FPdc, turn.

Row 3: Ch2, [2BPdc, 2FPdc] to last 2 sts, 2BPdc, turn.

Row 4: Rep Row 2.

All sizes:

Row 5: Ch3, 1dc in each st, turn.

Chevron section one

Row 6: Ch3 (does not count as a st throughout), 9 (12, 9, 12) (9, 12, 9) (12, 9, 12)dc, *ch2, sk 2 sts, 14dc* 3 (3, 4, 4) (5, 5, 6) (6, 7, 7) times, ch2, sk 2 sts, 9 (12, 9, 12) (9, 12, 9) (12, 9, 12)dc, turn.

Row 7: Ch3, 7 (10, 7, 10) (7, 10, 7) (10, 7, 10)dc, *ch2, sk 2 sts, 2dc, ch2, sk 2 sts, 10dc* 3 (3, 4, 4) (5, 5, 6) (6, 7, 7) times, ch2, sk 2 sts, 2dc, ch2, sk 2 sts, 7 (10, 7, 10) (7, 10, 7) (10, 7, 10)dc, turn.

Row 8: Ch3, 5 (8, 5, 8) (5, 8, 5) (8, 5, 8)dc, *ch2, sk 2 sts, 6dc* 7 (7, 9, 9) (11, 11, 13) (13, 15, 15) times, ch2, sk 2 sts, 5 (8, 5, 8) (5, 8, 5) (8, 5, 8)dc, turn.

Row 9: Ch3, 3 (6, 3, 6) (3, 6, 3) (6, 3, 6)dc, *ch2, sk 2 sts, 10dc, ch2, sk 2 sts, 2dc* 3 (3, 4, 4) (5, 5, 6) (6, 7, 7) times, ch2, sk 2 sts, 10dc, ch2, sk 2 sts, 3 (6, 3, 6) (3, 6, 3) (6, 3, 6)dc, turn.

Row 10: Ch3, 1 (4, 1, 4) (1, 4, 1) (4, 1, 4)dc, *ch2, sk 2 sts, 6dc* 8 (8, 10, 10) (12, 12, 14) (14, 16, 16) times, ch2, sk 2 sts, 1 (4, 1, 4) (1, 4, 1) (4, 1, 4)dc, turn.

Row 11: Rep Row 7.

Row 12: Rep Row 8.

Row 13: Rep Row 9.

Rep Rows 10–13 one (one, two, two) (two, two, two) (three, three, three) MORE times for a total of 17 (17, 21, 21) (21, 21, 21) (25, 25, 25) rows, then work Chevron Section Two.

Chevron section two

Row 14: Ch3, 1 (4, 1, 4) (1, 4, 1) (4, 1, 4)dc, *ch2, sk 2 sts, 6dc* 8 (8, 10, 10) (12, 12, 14) (14, 16, 16) times, ch2, sk 2 sts, 1 (4, 1, 4) (1, 4, 1) (4, 1, 4)dc, turn.

Row 15: Ch3, 7 (10, 7, 10) (7, 10, 7) (10, 7, 10)dc, *ch2, sk 2 sts, 2dc, ch2, sk 2 sts, 10dc* 3 (3, 4, 4) (5, 5, 6) (6, 7, 7) times, ch2, sk 2 sts, 2dc, ch2, sk 2 sts, 7 (10, 7, 10) (7, 10, 7) (10, 7, 10)dc, turn.

Row 16: Ch3, 5 (8, 5, 8) (5, 8, 5) (8, 5, 8)dc, *ch2, sk 2 sts, 6dc* 7 (7, 9, 9) (11, 11, 13) (13, 15, 15) times, ch2, sk 2 sts, 5 (8, 5, 8) (5, 8, 5) (8, 5, 8)dc, turn.

Row 17: Ch3, 3 (6, 3, 6) (3, 6, 3) (6, 3, 6)dc, *ch2, sk 2 sts, 10dc, ch2, sk 2 sts, 2dc* 3 (3, 4, 4) (5, 5, 6) (6, 7, 7) times, ch2, sk 2 sts, 10dc, ch2, sk 2 sts, 3 (6, 3, 6) (3, 6, 3) (6, 3, 6)dc, turn.

Row 18: Ch3, 9 (12, 9, 12) (9, 12, 9) (12, 9, 12)dc, *ch2, sk 2 sts, 14dc* 3 (3, 4, 4) (5, 5, 6) (6, 7, 7) times, ch2, sk 2 sts, 9 (12, 9, 12) (9, 12, 9) (12, 9, 12)dc, turn.

Row 19: Rep Row 15.

Row 20: Rep Row 16.

Row 21: Rep Row 17.

Rep Rows 18–21 one (one, one, one) (two, two, two) (two, two, two) MORE times for a total of 29 (29, 33, 33) (37, 37, 37) (41, 41, 41) rows, then work Chevron Section Three.

> **TIP:** You can easily alter the length of your piece by working additional or fewer Chevron Section One repeats.

Chevron section three

Row 22: Rep Row 18.

Row 23: Rep Row 15.

Row 24: Rep Row 16.

Row 25: Ch3, 1dc in each st, turn.

Rep Rows 22–25 one (two, two, two) (two, two, two) (two, two, two) MORE times for a total of 37 (41, 45, 45) (49, 49, 49) (53, 53, 53) rows, then work Chevron Section Four.

Chevron section four

Row 26: Rep Row 18.

Row 27: Rep Row 15.

Rows 28 and 29: Rep Row 25.

Rep Rows 26–29 once more for a total of 45 (49, 53, 53) (57, 57, 57) (61, 61, 61) rows.

Fasten off.

Front Panel

Work as per Back Panel until end of Chevron Section Three reps, then work Neckline One.

Neckline one

Sizes XXS (XS) only:

Row 1: Ch3, 9 (12)dc, ch2, sk 2 sts, 10 (10)dc, turn.

Row 2: Ch3, 8(8)dc, ch2, sk 2 sts, 2dc, ch2, sk 2 sts, 7 (10)dc, turn.

Sizes (S, M) (L, XL, 2X) (3X, 4X, 5X) only:

Row 1: Ch3, (9, 12) (9, 12, 9) (12, 9, 12)dc, *ch2, sk 2 sts, 14dc* (1, 1) (1, 1, 2) (2, 2, 2) times, ch2, sk 2 sts, (1, 1) (8, 8, 1) (1, 7, 7)dc, turn.

Sizes (S, M) only:

Row 2: Ch3, (3, 3)dc, ch2, sk 2 sts, *10dc, ch2, sk 2 sts, 2dc, ch2, sk 2 sts* once, (7, 10)dc, turn.

Sizes (L, XL) (4X, 5X) only:

Row 2: Ch3, (6, 6) (5, 5)dc, *ch2, sk 2 sts, 2dc, ch2, sk 2 sts, 10dc* (1, 1) (2, 2) times, ch2, sk 2 sts, 2dc, ch2, sk 2 sts, (7, 10) (7, 10)dc, turn.

Sizes (2X) (3X) only:

Row 2: Ch3, 3dc, *ch2, sk 2 sts, 10dc, ch2, sk 2 sts, 2dc* twice, ch2, sk 2 sts, (7) (10)dc, turn.

All sizes:

Row 3: Ch3, 1dc in each st, turn.

Row 4: Rep Row 3.

Rows 5–8: Rep Rows 1–4.

Row 9: Ch1, with RS of Front and Back Panels tog, 1sc through next 21 (24, 28, 31) (35, 38, 44) (47, 50, 53) sts on both edges to seam shoulder.

Fasten off.

Neckline two

Count 21 (24, 28, 31) (35, 38, 44) (47, 50, 53) sts from other edge of work and join yarn.

Sizes XXS (XS) only:

Row 1: Ch3, 10 (10)dc, ch2, sk 2 sts, 9 (12)dc, turn.

Row 2: Ch3, 7 (10)dc, ch2, sk 2 sts, 2dc, ch2, sk 2 sts, 8 (8)dc, turn.

Sizes (S, M) (L, XL, 2X) (3X, 4X, 5X) only:

Row 1: Ch3, (1, 1) (8, 8, 1) (1, 7, 7) dc, *ch2, sk 2 sts, 14dc* (1, 1) (1, 1, 2) (2, 2, 2) times, ch2, sk 2 sts, (9, 12) (9, 12, 9) (12, 9, 12)dc, turn.

Sizes (S, M) only:

Row 2: Ch3, (7, 10)dc, *ch2, sk 2 sts, 2dc, ch2, sk 2 sts, 10dc* once, ch2, sk 2 sts, (3, 3)dc, turn.

Sizes (L, XL) (4X, 5X) only:

Row 2: Ch3, (7, 10) (7, 10)dc, *ch2, sk 2 sts, 10dc, ch2, sk 2 sts, 2dc* (1, 1) (2, 2) times, ch2, sk 2 sts, 2dc, ch2, sk 2 sts, (6, 6) (5, 5)dc, turn.

Sizes (2X) (3X) only:

Row 2: Ch3, (7) (10)dc, *ch2, sk 2 sts, 2dc, ch2, sk 2 sts, 10dc* twice, ch2, sk 2 sts, 3dc, turn.

All sizes:

Row 3: Ch3, 1dc in each st, turn.

Row 4: Rep Row 3.

Rows 5–8: Rep Rows 1–4.

Row 9: Ch1, with RS of Front and Back Panels tog, 1sc through next 21 (24, 28, 31) (35, 38, 44) (47, 50, 53) sts on both edges to seam shoulder.

Fasten off.

Sleeves
(make two)

Round 1: Ch28 (28, 30, 30) (30, 30, 32) (32, 32, 34), ss to join into a ring.

Round 2 (RS): Ch3 (does not count as a st throughout), 1dc in each ch, ss to join.

Sizes XXS (XS) (2X) (3X, 4X) only:

Round 3: Ch2 (does not count as a st throughout), [2FPdc, 2BPdc] to last 3 sts, 2FPdc, 1BPdc, ss to join, do not turn.

Rounds 4–6: Rep Round 3.

Sizes (S, M) (L, XL) (5X) only:

Round 3: Ch2, [2FPdc, 2BPdc] to last st, 1FPdc, ss to join, do not turn.

Rounds 4–6: Rep Round 3.

Sizes XXS (XS, S) only:

Round 7: Ch3, 1dc in each of next 3 (1, 2) sts, 2dc in each of next 22 (26, 26) sts, 1dc in each of next 3 (1, 2) st(s), ss to join, turn. 50 (54, 56) sts

Sizes (M) (L, XL, 2X) (3X, 4X, 5X) only:

Round 7: Ch3, 3dc in each of next (1) (3, 4, 6) (8, 9, 8) sts, 2dc in each of next (14) (12, 11, 10) (8, 7, 9) sts, 3dc in each of next (1) (3, 4, 6) (8, 9, 8) sts, 2dc in each of next (14) (12, 11, 10) (8, 7, 9) sts, ss to join, turn. (62) (66, 68, 76) (80, 82, 84) sts

All sizes:

Round 8 (WS): Ch3, 24 (26, 27, 30) (32, 33, 37) (39, 40, 41)dc, ch2, sk 2 sts, 24 (26, 27, 30) (32, 33, 37) (39, 40, 41)dc, ss to join, turn.

Round 9: Ch3, 22 (24, 25, 28) (30, 31, 35) (37, 38, 39)dc, ch2, sk 2 sts, 2dc, ch2, sk 2 sts, 22 (24, 25, 28) (30, 31, 35) (37, 38, 39)dc, ss to join, turn.

Round 10: Ch3, 20 (22, 23, 26) (28, 29, 33) (35, 36, 37)dc, ch2, sk 2 sts, 6dc, ch2, sk 2 sts, 20 (22, 23, 26) (28, 29, 33) (35, 36, 37)dc, ss to join, turn.

Round 11: Ch3, 18 (20, 21, 24) (26, 27, 31) (33, 34, 35)dc, ch2, sk 2 sts, 10dc, ch2, sk 2 sts, 18 (20, 21, 24) (26, 27, 31) (33, 34, 35)dc, ss to join, turn.

Round 12: Ch3, 16 (18, 19, 22) (24, 25, 29) (31, 32, 33)dc, ch2, sk 2 sts, 6dc, ch2, sk 2 sts, 6dc, ch2, sk 2 sts, 16 (18, 19, 22) (24, 25, 29) (31, 32, 33)dc, ss to join, turn.

Round 13: Rep Round 9.

Round 14: Rep Round 10.

Round 15: Rep Round 11.

Rep Rounds 12–15 twice more for a total of 23 rounds.

Round 16: Rep Round 12.

Round 17: Rep Round 9.

Round 18: Rep Round 10.

Round 19: Rep Round 11.

Round 20: Rep Round 8.

Round 21: Rep Round 9.

Round 22: Rep Round 10.

Round 23: Rep Round 11.

Round 24: Rep Round 8.

Round 25: Rep Round 9.

Round 26: Rep Round 10.

Round 27: Ch3, 1dc in each st, ss to join, turn.

Rep Rounds 24–27 once more for a total of 39 rounds.

Sizes XXS (XS) only:

Fasten off.

All other sizes:

Round 28: Rep Round 8.

Round 29: Rep Round 9.

Round 30: Rep Round 27.

Round 31: Rep Round 27.

Fasten off.

Finishing

Seam sides and join Sleeves to body panels.

Neckline edging

With RS facing, join yarn in a central st at back of neckline.

TIP: As your body panels are worked in turned rows there is no RS or WS, so just choose your favourite when seaming!

Round 1: Ch3, 1dc in each st at back of neckline, 2dc in each neckline row end, 1dc in each st at front of neckline, 2dc in each neckline row end as before, 1dc in each rem st to ch-3, ss to join, do not turn.

Round 2: Ch2, [2FPdc, 2BPdc] around, ss to join, do not turn.

Round 3: Rep Round 2.

Round 4: Rep Round 2.

Fasten off and weave in all rem ends.

BOBBLE & CHIC CARDIGAN

A fun and funky cardigan using a mix of bobbles and filet for a unique look. The colour changes can feel a bit daunting, but once you're in the swing of it you'll be happily hooking away with ease. The Bobble & Chic Cardigan is designed to be slightly cropped, but you can easily adjust the length to suit your personal style by working more or fewer repeats.

Gauge (tension)

16 sts x 9 rows = 10 x 10cm (4 x 4in) using 4mm (US size G/6) hook.

Yarn & hook

Paintbox Yarns Simply DK (100% acrylic), DK (light worsted) weight yarn, 276m (302yd) per 100g (3½oz) ball in the following shades:

- Vanilla Cream (107) MC: 3½ (4, 4¾, 5) (5½, 6¼, 7) (7¼, 8¼, 8¾) balls
- Daffodil Yellow (121); Spearmint Green (125); Tea Rose (142); Summer Sky Blue (63): ½ (½, ½, ½) (¾, ¾, ¾) (¾, 1, 1) ball of each CC

4mm (US size G/6) crochet hook

	XXS	XS	S	M	L	XL	2X	3X	4X	5X
Circumference	84cm (33in)	89cm (35in)	104cm (41in)	111cm (43¾in)	124cm (48¾in)	129cm (50¾in)	144cm (56¾in)	151cm (59¼in)	164cm (64½in)	169cm (66½in)
Length	43cm (17in)	51cm (20in)	51cm (20in)	51cm (20in)	51cm (20in)	58cm (22¾in)	58cm (22¾in)	58cm (22¾in)	66cm (26in)	66cm (26in)
Sleeve depth	16cm (6¼in)	16.5cm (6½in)	18cm (7in)	20.5cm (8in)	20.5cm (8in)	22cm (8¾in)	23cm (9in)	24cm (9½in)	25cm (9¾in)	27cm (10½in)

Pattern notes & chart

The order in which you use contrast colours can really change the finish of this cardigan. Work them diagonally as shown, in rows for an ombre look, or go for one colour bobble all over for a more subtle design.

Chart shows pattern repeat for guidance on stitch placement within the filet section only, place repeats within rows or rounds following written instructions for your chosen size. Read RS (even-number) rows from left to right and WS (odd-number) rows from right to left.

Special abbreviation

Bobble: [yo, insert hook into st, yo, pull through st, yo, pull through 2 loops on hook] 4 times, yo, pull through all remaining loops on hook

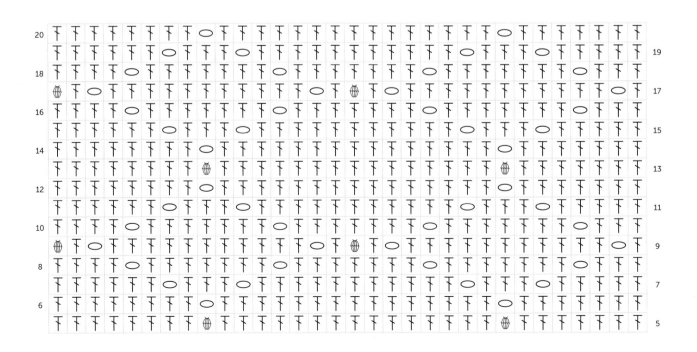

Back Panel

Row 1: Using MC, fdc67 (71, 83, 89) (99, 103, 115) (121, 131, 135), turn.

OR: Using MC, ch70 (74, 86, 92) (102, 106, 118) (124, 134, 138), 1dc in fourth ch from hook and each ch along, turn.

Row 2: Ch3 (does not count as a st throughout), [1FPdc, 1BPdc] to last st, 1FPdc, turn.

Rows 3 and 4: Rep Row 2.

NOTE: All bobbles are worked in one of four CCs; change yarn during the final yarn over of the previous stitch, fasten off after each bobble and weave in ends as you go.

Row 5 (WS): Ch3, 9 (11, 9, 12) (9, 11, 9) (12, 9, 11)dc, *bobble, 15dc* 3 (3, 4, 4) (5, 5, 6) (6, 7, 7) times, bobble, 9 (11, 9, 12) (9, 11, 9) (12, 9, 11)dc, turn.

Row 6 (RS): Ch3, 9 (11, 9, 12) (9, 11, 9) (12, 9, 11)dc, *ch1, sk 1 st, 15dc* 3 (3, 4, 4) (5, 5, 6) (6, 7, 7) times, ch1, sk 1 st, 9 (11, 9, 12) (9, 11, 9) (12, 9, 11)dc, turn.

Row 7: Ch3, 7 (9, 7, 10) (7, 9, 7) (10, 7, 9)dc, *ch1, sk 1 st, 3dc, ch1, sk 1 st, 11dc* 3 (3, 4, 4) (5, 5, 6) (6, 7, 7) times, ch1, sk 1 st, 3dc, ch1, sk 1 st, 7 (9, 7, 10) (7, 9, 7) (10, 7, 9)dc, turn.

Row 8: Ch3, 5 (7, 5, 8) (5, 7, 5) (8, 5, 7)dc, *ch1, sk 1 st, 7dc* 7 (7, 9, 9) (11, 11, 13) (13, 15, 15) times, ch1, sk 1 st, 5 (7, 5, 8) (5, 7, 5) (8, 5, 7)dc, turn.

Row 9: Ch3, 1 (3, 1, 4) (1, 3, 1) (4, 1, 3)dc, *bobble, 1dc, ch1, sk 1 st, 11dc, ch1, sk 1 st, 1dc* 4 (4, 5, 5) (6, 6, 7) (7, 8, 8) times, bobble, 1 (3, 1, 4) (1, 3, 1) (4, 1, 3)dc, turn.

Row 10: Rep Row 8.

Row 11: Rep Row 7.

Row 12: Rep Row 6.

TIP: You can add more repeats before the Final Row on both the Front and the Back Panels if you need additional length.

Rep Rows 5–12 four (five, five, five) (five, six, six) (six, seven, seven) MORE times for a total of 44 (52, 52, 52) (52, 60, 60) (60, 68, 68) rows or until 2cm (¾in) short of desired length, then rep Row 5 once more.

Final row: Ch3, 1dc in each st.

Fasten off.

Front Panels
(make two)

Row 1: Fdc25 (27, 35, 35) (41, 43, 51) (51, 55, 57), turn.

OR: Ch28 (30, 38, 38) (44, 46, 54) (54, 58, 60), 1dc in fourth ch from hook and each ch along, turn.

Row 2: Ch3, [1FPdc, 1BPdc] to last st, 1FPdc, turn.

Rows 3 and 4: Rep Row 2.

Sizes XXS (XS) only:

Row 5 (WS): Ch3, 12 (13)dc, bobble, 12 (13)dc, turn.

Row 6 (RS): Ch3, 12 (13)dc, ch1, sk 1 st, 12 (13)dc, turn.

Row 7: Ch3, 10 (11)dc, ch1, sk 1 st, 3dc, ch1, sk 1 st, 10 (11)dc, turn.

All other sizes:

Row 5 (WS): Ch3, (9, 9) (12, 13, 9) (9, 11, 12)dc, *bobble, 15dc* (1, 1) (1, 1, 2) (2, 2, 2) times, bobble, (9, 9) (12, 13, 9) (9, 11, 12)dc, turn.

Row 6 (RS): Ch3, (9, 9) (12, 13, 9) (9, 11, 12)dc, *ch1, sk 1 st, 15dc* (1, 1) (1, 1, 2) (2, 2, 2) times, ch1, sk 1 st, (9, 9) (12, 13, 9) (9, 11, 12)dc, turn.

Row 7: Ch3, (7, 7) (10, 11, 7) (7, 9, 10)dc, *ch1, sk 1 st, 3dc, ch1, sk 1 st, 11dc* (1, 1) (1, 1, 2) (2, 2, 2) times, ch1, sk 1 st, 3dc, ch1, sk 1 st, (7, 7) (10, 11, 7) (7, 9, 10)dc, turn.

All sizes:

Row 8: Ch3, 8 (9, 5, 5) (8, 9, 5) (5, 7, 8)dc, *ch1, sk 1 st, 7dc* 1 (1, 3, 3) (3, 3, 5) (5, 5, 5) times, ch1, sk 1 st, 8 (9, 5, 5) (8, 9, 5) (5, 7, 8)dc, turn.

Row 9: Ch3, 4 (5, 1, 1) (4, 5, 1) (1, 3, 4)dc, *bobble, 1dc, ch1, sk 1 st, 11dc, ch1, sk 1 st, 1dc* 1 (1, 2, 2) (2, 2, 3) (3, 3, 3) times, bobble, 4 (5, 1, 1) (4, 5, 1) (1, 3, 4)dc, turn.

Row 10: Rep Row 8.

Row 11: Rep Row 7.

Row 12: Rep Row 6.

Rep Rows 5–12 four (five, five, five) (five, six, six) (six, seven, seven) MORE times for a total of 44 (52, 52, 52) (52, 60, 60) (60, 68, 68) rows or until 2 rows short of Back Panel, then rep Row 5 once more.

Final row: Ch3, 1dc in each st, turn.

Seaming row: With RS of Back and one Front Panel tog, 1sc through each of next 25 (27, 35, 35) (41, 43, 51) (51, 55, 57) sts on both edges to seam shoulder.

Fasten off.

Rep Seaming Row with second Front Panel.

Sleeves

(make two)

Round 1: Ch30 (30, 30, 32) (32, 32, 32) (34, 34, 34), ss to join into a ring.

Round 2: Ch3 (does not count as a st throughout), 1dc in each ch, ss to join, do not turn.

Round 3: Ch2, [1FPdc, 1BPdc] around, ss to join, do not turn.

Rounds 4 and 5: Rep Row 2.

Sizes XXS (XS, S) only:

Round 6: Ch3, 1dc in each of next 4 (3, 1) dc, 2dc in each of next 11 (13, 17) sts, 1dc in each of next 5 (4, 2) dc, 2dc in each of next 10 sts, ss to join, turn. 51 (53, 57) sts

Size (M) only:

Round 6: Ch3, 2dc in each st to last st, 1dc in final st, ss to join, turn. (63) sts

Size (L) only:

Round 6: Ch3, 3dc in first st, 2dc in each st around, ss to join, turn. (65) sts

Sizes (XL, 2X) (3X, 4X, 5X) only:

Round 6: Ch3, 2dc in each of next (13, 11) (12, 11, 8) sts, 3dc in each of next (2, 4) (4, 5, 9) sts, 2dc in each of next (14, 12) (13, 12, 8) sts, 3dc in each of next (3, 5) (5, 6, 8) sts, ss to join, turn. (69, 73) (77, 79, 83) sts

All sizes:

Round 7 (WS): Ch3, 9 (10, 12, 15) (16, 10, 12) (14, 15, 9)dc, *bobble, 15dc* 2 (2, 2, 2) (2, 3, 3) (3, 3, 4) times, bobble, 9 (10, 12, 15) (16, 10, 12) (14, 15, 9)dc, ss to join, turn.

Round 8 (RS): Ch3, 9 (10, 12, 15) (16, 10, 12) (14, 15, 9)dc, *ch1, sk 1 st, 15dc* 2 (2, 2, 2) (2, 3, 3) (3, 3, 4) times, ch1, sk 1 st, 9 (10, 12, 15) (16, 10, 12) (14, 15, 9)dc, ss to join, turn.

Round 9: Ch3, 7 (8, 10, 13) (14, 8, 10) (12, 13, 7)dc, *ch1, sk 1 st, 3dc, ch1, sk 1 st, 11dc* 2 (2, 2, 2) (2, 3, 3) (3, 3, 4) times, ch1, sk 1 st, 3dc, ch1, sk 1 st, 7 (8, 10, 13) (14, 8, 10) (12, 13, 7)dc, ss to join, turn.

Round 10: Ch3, 5 (6, 8, 11) (12, 6, 8) (10, 11, 5)dc, *ch1, sk 1 st, 7dc* 5 (5, 5, 5) (5, 7, 7) (7, 7, 9) times, ch1, sk 1 st, 5 (6, 8, 11) (12, 6, 8) (10, 11, 5)dc, ss to join, turn.

Round 11: Ch3, 1 (2, 4, 7) (8, 2, 4) (6, 7, 1)dc, *bobble, 1dc, ch1, sk 1 st, 11dc, ch1, sk 1 st, 1dc* 3 (3, 3, 3) (3, 4, 4) (4, 4, 5) times, bobble, 1 (2, 4, 7) (8, 2, 4) (6, 7, 1)dc, ss to join, turn.

Round 12: Rep Round 10.

Round 13: Rep Round 9.

Round 14: Rep Round 8.

Rep Rounds 7–14 four MORE times for a total of 46 rounds or until desired length, then rep Round 7 once more.

Final round: Ch3, 1dc in each st, ss to join.

Fasten off.

Finishing

Seam sides and join Sleeves to body panels.

Edging

With RS facing, join yarn in Row 1 end on left front panel.

Row 1: Ch1, 2sc in each row end along left Front Panel, 1sc in each st at back of neckline, 2sc in each row end along right Front Panel, turn.

Row 2: Ch1, 1sc in each st.

Fasten off and weave in all ends.

LAZY WAVES SWEATER

A mix of stitches creates soothing waves across a summer-friendly make. The dropped hem adds a quirky twist to an otherwise simple shape. A pleasure to make but even more enjoyable to wear, this sweater will be a staple piece in your wardrobe for years to come.

Gauge (tension)

16 sts x 9 dc rows/12 rows over patt = 10 x 10cm (4 x 4in) using 4mm (US size G/6) hook.

Yarn & hook

Paintbox Yarns Simply DK (100% acrylic), DK (light worsted) weight yarn, 276m (302yd) per 100g (3½oz) ball in the following shade:
• Summer Sky Blue (63): 3 (3¾, 4¼, 4½) (5, 5¼, 6) (6¾, 7½, 7¾) balls

4mm (US size G/6) crochet hook

2 stitch markers

	XXS	XS	S	M	L	XL	2X	3X	4X	5X
Circumference	82.5cm (32½in)	90cm (35½in)	102.5cm (40¼in)	110cm (43½in)	122.5cm (48¼in)	130cm (51¼in)	142cm (56in)	150cm (59in)	162.5cm (64in)	170cm (67in)
Length at back	48cm (19in)	55.5cm (21¾in)	55.5cm (21¾in)	55.5cm (21¾in)	55.5cm (21¾in)	55.5cm (21¾in)	55.5cm (21¾in)	62cm (24½in)	62cm (24½in)	62cm (24½in)
Length at front	41cm (16¼in)	49cm (19¼in)	49cm (19¼in)	49cm (19¼in)	49cm (19¼in)	49cm (19¼in)	49cm (19¼in)	55.5cm (21¾in)	55.5cm (21¾in)	55.5cm (21¾in)
Sleeve depth	16cm (6¼in)	17cm (6¾in)	18cm (7in)	20cm (8in)	21cm (8¼in)	22cm (8¾in)	24cm (9½in)	25cm (9¾in)	26cm (10¼in)	27cm (10½in)

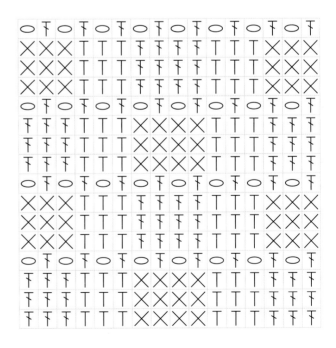

Pattern notes & chart

You can alter the length of your piece by working additional or fewer repeats.

Chart shows pattern repeat for guidance on stitch placement within the filet section only and does not have row or stitch numbers because it shows different areas of pattern on one chart. Place repeats within rows or rounds following written instructions for your chosen size.

TIP: This pattern is designed with a drop hem at the back, but if you prefer it without simply work one less Little Waves repeat on the Back Panel.

Back Panel

Row 1: Fdc60 (66, 76, 82) (92, 98, 108) (114, 124, 130), turn.

OR: Ch63 (69, 79, 85) (95, 101, 111) (117, 127, 133), 1dc in fourth ch from hook and each ch along, turn.

Row 2: Ch3 (does not count as a st throughout), 2dc in first st, 1dc in each st to last st, 2dc in final st, turn. 62 (68, 78, 84) (94, 100, 110) (116, 126, 132) sts

Rows 3 and 4: Rep Row 2. 66 (72, 82, 88) (98, 104, 114) (120, 130, 136) sts

Little waves

Row 5 (RS): Ch3, 4 (7, 4, 7) (4, 7, 4) (7, 4, 7)dc, *3hdc, 4sc, 3hdc, 6dc* 3 (3, 4, 4) (5, 5, 6) (6, 7, 7) times, 3hdc, 4sc, 3hdc, 4 (7, 4, 7) (4, 7, 4) (7, 4, 7)dc, turn.

Rows 6 and 7: Rep Row 5.

Row 8: Ch3, 2dc, *ch1, sk 1 st, 1dc* to end, turn.

Row 9: Ch1, 4 (7, 4, 7) (4, 7, 4) (7, 4, 7)sc, *3hdc, 4dc, 3hdc, 6sc* 3 (3, 4, 4) (5, 5, 6) (6, 7, 7) times, 3hdc, 4dc, 3hdc, 4 (7, 4, 7) (4, 7, 4) (7, 4, 7)sc, turn.

Rows 10 and 11: Rep Row 9.

Row 12: Rep Row 8.

Rep Rows 5–12 three (four, four, four) (four, four, four) (five, five, five) MORE times then rep Rows 5–8 once more for a total of 40 (48, 48, 48) (48, 48, 48) (56, 56, 56) rows.

Big wave

Rows 13–17: Rep Row 9.

Row 18: Rep Row 8.

Rows 19 and 20: Rep Row 5.

Row 21: Ch3, 1dc in each st, turn.

Rep Row 21 four (five, five, five) (five, five, five) (five, five, five) MORE times for a total of 13 (14, 14, 14) (14, 14, 14) (14, 14, 14) rows here and 53 (62, 62, 62) (62, 62, 62) (70, 70, 70) rows overall.

Fasten off.

Front Panel

Rows 1–12: Work as per Back Panel.

Rep Rows 5–12 two (three, three, three) (three, three, three) (four, four, four) MORE times then rep Rows 5–8 once more for a total of 32 (40, 40, 40) (40, 40, 40) (48, 48, 48) rows.

Front big wave

Rows 13–17: Rep Row 9.

Row 18: Rep Row 8.

Rows 19 and 20: Rep Row 5.

Row 21: Ch3, 1dc in each st.

Neckline one

Row 1: Ch3, 20 (23, 28, 30) (35, 38, 43) (45, 50, 53)dc, turn.

Row 2: Ch3, 1dc in each st, turn.

Rows 3 and 4: Rep Row 2.

Size XXS only:

Move on to Row 6.

All other sizes:

Row 5: Rep Row 2.

All sizes:

Row 6: Ch1, with RS of Front and Back Panels tog, 1sc through next 20 (23, 28, 30) (35, 38, 43) (45, 50, 53) sts on both pieces to seam shoulder.

Fasten off.

Neckline two

Count 20 (23, 28, 30) (35, 38, 43) (45, 50, 53) sts from other edge of work and join yarn.

Row 1: Ch3, 20 (23, 28, 30) (35, 38, 43) (45, 50, 53)dc, turn.

Row 2: Ch3, 1dc in each st, turn.

Rows 3 and 4: Rep Row 2.

Size XXS only:

Move on to Row 6.

All other sizes:

Row 5: Rep Row 2.

All sizes:

Row 6: Ch1, with RS of Front and Back Panels tog, 1sc through next 20 (23, 28, 30) (35, 38, 43) (45, 50, 53) sts on both pieces to seam shoulder.

Fasten off.

Sleeves
(make two)

NOTE: See sizing table for finished sleeve depths and work size that suits you best.

Row 1 (RS): Fdc38 (38, 42, 42) (42, 42, 46) (46, 48, 48), turn.

OR: Ch41 (41, 45, 45) (45, 45, 49) (49, 51, 51), 1dc in fourth ch from hook and each ch along, turn.

Row 2 (WS): Ch3 (does not count as a st throughout), 2dc in first st, 1dc in each st to last st, 2dc in final st, turn. 40 (40, 44, 44) (44, 44, 48) (48, 50, 50) sts

Row 3: Rep Row 2. 42 (42, 46, 46) (46, 46, 50) (50, 52, 52) sts

Row 4: Ch3, 2dc in first st, 20 (20, 23, 23) (23, 23, 25) (25, 26, 26)dc, place marker in last st worked, 1dc in each st to last st, 2dc in final st, ss to join.

Fasten off.

Turn, and join yarn in marked st.

NOTE: This is so cuff split will sit at outside of sleeve and seam will be underneath.

Round 5: Ch3, 1dc in each st, ss to join, turn. 44 (44, 48, 48) (48, 48, 52) (52, 54, 54) sts

Work foll IR, DIR and MR rounds as instructed for a total of 24 (26, 26, 26) (26, 26, 28) (28, 28, 28) rounds and 52 (54, 58, 64) (68, 70, 76) (80, 84, 84) sts.

Fasten off at end of final round.

Inc round (IR): Ch3, 2dc in first st, 1dc in each rem st, ss to join, turn. (+1 st)

Double inc round (DIR): Ch3, 2dc in first st, 1dc in each st to last st, 2dc in final st, ss to join, turn. (+2 sts)

Maintenance round (MR): Ch3, 1dc in each st, ss to join, turn. (+0 sts)

Size XXS only

Round 6: IR.

Round 7: MR.

Rounds 8–21: Rep Rounds 6 and 7.

Rounds 22–24: MR.

Size (XS, S) only

Round 6: IR.

Round 7: MR.

Rounds 8–25: Rep Rounds 6 and 7.

Round 26: MR.

Size (M) only

Rounds 6–8: IR.

Round 9: MR.

Rounds 10–25: Rep Rounds 6–9.

Round 26: IR.

Size (L) only

Round 6: MR.

Rounds 7–26: IR.

Size (XL) only

Round 6: DIR.

Rounds 7–26: IR.

Size (2X) only

Round 6: DIR.

Rounds 7–28: IR.

Size (3X) only

Round 6: DIR.

Rounds 7–10: IR.

Rounds 11–25: Rep Rounds 6–10.

Round 26: DIR.

Rounds 27 and 28: IR.

Size (4X) only

Round 6: DIR.

Rounds 7 and 8: IR.

Rounds 9–26: Rep Rounds 6–8.

Rounds 27 and 28: IR.

Size (5X) only

Round 6: DIR.

Rounds 7 and 8: IR.

Rounds 9–26: Rep Rounds 6–8.

Rounds 27 and 28: DIR.

Finishing

Sleeve edging

With RS facing, join yarn in any st by join at cuff.

Round 1: Ch1, 1sc in each st around bottom edge of Sleeve, at cuff split work 2sc in each split row end, ss into seam, then work 2sc in each split row end as before, cont to sc along Sleeve edge to ch-1, ss to join.

Fasten off.

Seaming

Lay body panels flat with WS facing. Lay Sleeve next to body panels and place marker where Sleeve join meets body. Find Front Panel Row 8 end (first filet row) and place marker through to join with row that sits level with this on Back Panel. Seam sides from here up to Sleeve marker, then join Sleeves to body panels.

Neckline edging

With RS facing, join yarn in any st at back of neckline.

Round 1: Ch3, 1dc in each st along back of neckline, 2dc in each Neckline One row end, then 1dc in each st at front of neckline, 2dc in each Neckline Two row end, then 1dc in each rem st to ch-3, ss to join, do not turn.

Round 2: Ch1, 1sc in each st, ss to join.

Fasten off.

Bottom edging

With RS facing, join yarn in any st at back of work.

Round 1: Ch1, 1sc in each st around bottom edge of work to side split, 2sc in each split row end, ss in seam, 2sc in each split row end as before, cont 1sc in each st along bottom edge. Rep as set for second split, then 1sc to ch-1, ss to join.

Fasten off and weave in all ends.

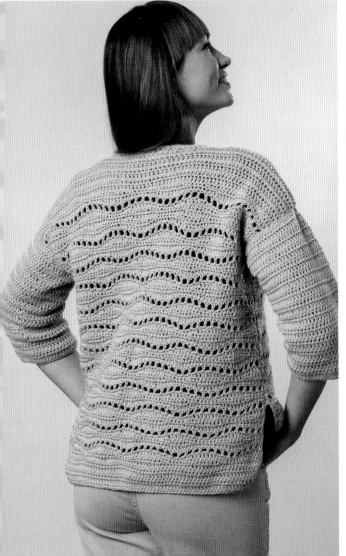

COTTON CANDY CARDIGAN

A cute and cosy cardigan for spring evenings or trips to the fair, your Cotton Candy Cardigan is a super simple and versatile make to keep the sea breeze away. The pretty repeats work up quickly and easily giving a subtle nod to filet within basic stitches. Make this one in a sugary sweet pink for a fun and versatile cover up.

Gauge (tension)

13 sts x 7 rows = 10 x 10cm (4 x 4in) using 5mm (US size H/8) hook.

Yarn & hook

Paintbox Yarns Simply Aran (100% acrylic), aran (worsted) weight yarn, 184m (201yd) per 100g (3½oz) ball in the following shade:
• Dusty Rose (241): 3¼ (3¾, 4½, 5) (5½, 5½, 6¼) (7¼, 7¾, 8) balls

5mm (US size H/8) crochet hook

	XXS	XS	S	M	L	XL	2X	3X	4X	5X
Circumference	77cm (30¼in)	83cm (32¾in)	95.5cm (37½in)	101.5cm (40in)	114cm (45in)	120cm (47¼in)	132cm (52in)	138.5cm (54½in)	151cm (59¼in)	157cm (61¾in)
Length	44cm (17¼in)	53cm (21in)	53cm (21in)	53cm (21in)	53cm (21in)	53cm (21in)	53cm (21in)	61cm (24in)	61cm (24in)	61cm (24in)
Sleeve depth	14cm (5½in)	15cm (6in)	17cm (6¾in)	19cm (7½in)	19cm (7½in)	20cm (8in)	22cm (8¾in)	24cm (9½in)	24cm (9½in)	25cm (9¾in)

Pattern notes & chart

As your body panels are worked in turned rows there is no right or wrong side, so just choose your favourite when seaming!

Chart shows pattern repeat for guidance on stitch placement within the filet section only, place repeats within rows or rounds following written instructions for your chosen size. Read odd-number rows from right to left and even-number rows from left to right.

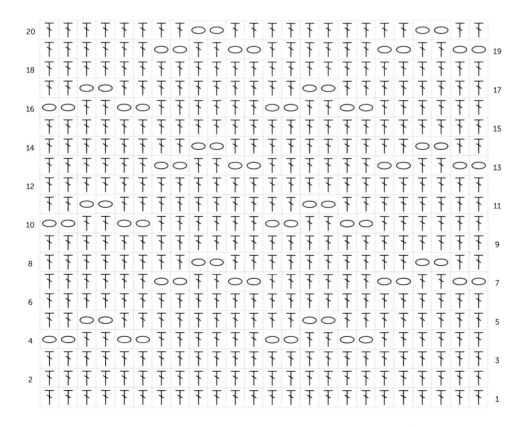

Back Panel

Row 1: Fdc50 (54, 62, 66) (74, 78, 86) (90, 98, 102), turn.

OR: Ch53 (57, 65, 69) (77, 81, 89) (93, 101, 105), 1dc in fourth ch from hook and each ch along, turn.

Row 2: Ch3 (does not count as a st throughout), 1dc in each st, turn.

Row 3: Rep Row 2.

Row 4: Ch3, 4 (6, 4, 6) (4, 6, 4) (6, 4, 6)dc, *ch2, sk 2 sts, 2dc, ch2, sk 2 sts, 6dc* to last 10 (12, 10, 12) (10, 12, 10) (12, 10, 12) sts, ch2, sk 2 sts, 2dc, ch2, sk 2 sts, 1dc in each rem st, turn.

Row 5: Ch3, 6 (8, 6, 8) (6, 8, 6) (8, 6, 8)dc, *ch2, sk 2 sts, 10dc* to last 8 (10, 8, 10) (8, 10, 8) (10, 8, 10) sts, ch2, sk 2 sts, 1dc in each rem st, turn.

Row 6: Ch3, 1dc in each st, turn.

Row 7: Ch3, 10 (12, 10, 12) (10, 12, 10) (12, 10, 12)dc, *ch2, sk 2 sts, 2dc, ch2, sk 2 sts, 6dc* to last 4 (6, 4, 6) (4, 6, 4) (6, 4, 6) sts, 1dc in each rem st, turn.

Row 8: Ch3, 12 (14, 12, 14) (12, 14, 12) (14, 12, 14)dc, *ch2, sk 2 sts, 10dc* to last 2 (4, 2, 4) (2, 4, 2) (4, 2, 4) sts, 1dc in each rem st, turn.

Row 9: Ch3, 1dc in each st, turn.

Rep Rows 4–9 three (four, four, four) (four, four, four) (five, five, five) MORE times, then rep Rows 4–6 once more and then Row 6 one final time for a total of 31 (37, 37, 37) (37, 37, 37) (43, 43, 43) rows.

Fasten off.

Front Panels

(make two)

Row 1: Fdc20 (22, 26, 28) (32, 32, 38) (38, 42, 44), turn.

OR: Ch23 (25, 29, 31) (35, 35, 41) (41, 45, 47), 1dc in fourth ch from hook and each ch along, turn.

Row 2: Ch3 (does not count as a st throughout), 1dc in each st, turn.

Row 3: Rep Row 2.

> **TIP:** You can easily adjust the length of your cardi by working more or fewer repeats. Add a strand of mohair to your work for extra cotton candy fluff!

Sizes XXS (XS) only:

Row 4: Ch3, 7 (8)dc, ch2, sk 2 sts, 2dc, ch2, sk 2 sts, 7 (8)dc, turn.

Row 5: Ch3, 9 (10)dc, ch2, sk 2 sts, 9 (10)dc, turn.

Row 6: Ch3, 1dc in each st, turn.

Rep Rows 4–6 eight (ten) MORE times, then rep Row 6 once more for a total of 31 (37) rows.

Seaming row: Ch1, with RS of Back and one Front Panel tog, 1sc through next 20 (22) sts on both edges to seam shoulder.

Fasten off.

Repeat Seaming Row with second Front Panel.

Sizes (S, M) (L, XL) only:

Row 4: Ch3, (4, 5) (7, 7)dc, *ch2, sk 2 sts, 2dc, ch2, sk 2 sts, 6dc* once, ch2, sk 2 sts, 2dc, ch2, sk 2 sts, (4, 5) (7, 7)dc, turn.

Row 5: Ch3, (6, 7) (9, 9)dc, *ch2, sk 2 sts, 10dc* once, ch2, sk 2 sts, (6, 7) (9, 9)dc, turn.

Row 6: Ch3, 1dc in each st, turn.

Row 7: Ch3, (10, 11) (13, 13) dc, ch2, sk 2 sts, 2dc, ch2, sk 2 sts, (10, 11) (13, 13)dc, turn.

Row 8: Ch3, (12, 13) (15, 15)dc, ch2, sk 2 sts, (12, 13) (15, 15)dc, turn.

Row 9: Ch3, 1dc in each st, turn.

Rep Rows 4–9 (4, 4) (4, 4) MORE times, then rep Rows 4–6 once more and then Row 6 one final time for a total of (37, 37) (37, 37) rows.

Seaming row: Ch1, with RS of Back and one Front Panel tog, 1sc through next (26, 28) (32, 32) sts on both edges to seam shoulder.

Fasten off.

Rep Seaming Row with second Front Panel.

Sizes (2X) (3X, 4X, 5X) only:

Row 4: Ch3, (4) (4, 6, 7)dc, *ch2, sk 2 sts, 2dc, ch2, sk 2 sts, 6dc* to last (10) (10, 12, 13) sts, ch2, sk 2 sts, 2dc, ch2, sk 2 sts, 1dc in each rem st, turn.

Row 5: Ch3, (6) (6, 8, 9)dc, *ch2, sk 2 sts, 10dc* to last (8) (8, 10, 11) sts, ch2, sk 2 sts, 1dc in each rem st, turn.

Row 6: Ch3, 1dc in each st, turn.

Row 7: Ch3, (10) (10, 12, 13) dc, *ch2, sk 2 sts, 2dc, ch2, sk 2 sts, 6dc* to last (4) (4, 6, 7) sts, 1dc in each rem st, turn.

Row 8: Ch3, (12) (12, 14, 15)dc, *ch2, sk 2 sts, 10dc* to last (2) (2, 4, 5) sts, 1dc in each rem st, turn.

Row 9: Ch3, 1dc in each st, turn.

Rep Rows 4–9 (4) (5, 5, 5) MORE times, then rep Rows 4–6 one more time and then Row 6 one final time for a total of (37) (43, 43, 43) rows.

Seaming row: Ch1, with RS of Back and one Front Panel tog, 1sc through next (38) (38, 42, 44) sts on both edges to seam shoulder.

Fasten off.

Rep Seaming Row with second Front Panel.

Sleeves

(make two)

Round 1: Ch20 (22, 24, 25) (25, 25, 26) (28, 28, 28), ss to join, turn.

Round 2: Ch3 (does not count as a st throughout), 1dc in each st, ss to join, turn.

Rounds 3 and 4: Rep Round 2.

Sizes XXS (XS, S) only:

Round 5: Ch3, 3 (5, 5)dc, 2dc in each rem st, ss to join, turn. 37 (39, 43) sts

Sizes (M) (L) only:

Round 5: Ch3, 1dc, 2dc in each rem st, ss to join, turn. (49) (49) sts

Sizes (XL, 2X) (3X, 4X, 5X) only:

Round 5: Ch3, 2dc in each of next (12, 10) (11, 11, 10) sts, 3dc in each of next (1, 5) (5, 5, 7) sts, 2dc in each of next (12, 11) (12, 12, 11) sts, ss to join, turn. (51, 57) (61, 61, 63) sts

All sizes:

Round 6: Ch3, 3 (4, 6, 3) (3, 4, 7) (3, 3, 4)dc, *ch2, sk 2 sts, 2dc, ch2, sk 2 sts, 6dc* to last 10 (11, 13, 10) (10, 11, 14) (10, 10, 11) sts, ch2, sk 2 sts, 2dc, ch2, sk 2 sts, 1dc in each rem st, ss to join, turn.

Round 7: Ch3, 6 (7, 9, 6) (6, 7, 10) (6, 6, 7)dc, *ch2, sk 2 sts, 10dc* to last 7 (8, 10, 7) (7, 8, 11) (7, 7, 8) sts, ch2, sk 2 sts, 1dc in each rem st, ss to join, turn.

Round 8: Ch3, 1dc in each st, ss to join, turn.

Round 9: Ch3, 10 (11, 13, 10) (10, 11, 14) (10, 10, 11)dc, *ch2, sk 2 sts, 2dc, ch2, sk 2 sts, 6dc* to last 3 (4, 6, 3) (3, 4, 7) (3, 4, 4) sts, 1dc in each rem st, ss to join, turn.

Round 10: Ch3, 11 (12, 14, 11) (11, 12, 15) (11, 11, 12)dc, *ch2, sk 2 sts, 10dc* to last 14 (15, 17, 14) (14, 15, 18) (14, 14, 15) sts, ch2, sk 2 sts, 1dc in each rem st, ss to join, turn.

Round 11: Ch3, 1dc in each st, ss to join, turn.

Size XXS only

Rep Rounds 6–11 twice more, then rep Rounds 6–8 one more time.

Fasten off.

All other sizes:

Rep Rounds 6–11 three more times.

Fasten off.

Finishing

Seam sides and join Sleeves to body panels.

Edging

With RS facing, join yarn in Row 1 end on left Front panel.

Row 1: Ch1, 2sc in each row end along left Front Panel, 1sc in each st at back of neckline, then 2sc in each row end on right Front Panel, turn.

Row 2: Ch1, 1sc in each st from prev row, rotate to work along bottom edge, 1sc in each st along bottom edge, ss to ch-1 to join.

Fasten off and weave in all ends.

CHECKERBOARD SWEATER

A great example of how effective a simple filet repeat can look. Meditative repeats create eye-catching geometric shapes within a snuggly aran (worsted) sweater. The turtleneck is perfect for autumn and the dropped hem adds an extra touch of sass. Brace yourself for compliments when you wear this one, it always draws attention!

Gauge (tension)

13 sts x 7 rows = 10 x 10cm (4 x 4in) using 5mm (US size H/8) hook.

Yarn & hook

Paintbox Yarns Simply Aran (100% acrylic), aran (worsted) weight yarn, 184m (201yd) per 100g (3½oz) ball in the following shade:
- Spearmint Green (232): 4½ (4¾, 5½, 6½) (6¾, 7¼, 8¾) (9½, 9¾, 10½) balls

5mm (US size H/8) crochet hook

2 stitch markers

	XXS	XS	S	M	L	XL	2X	3X	4X	5X
Circumference	85cm (33½in)	88cm (34¾in)	100cm (39¼in)	112cm (44in)	118.5cm (46¾in)	131cm (51½in)	140cm (55in)	155.5cm (61¼in)	162cm (63¾in)	171cm (67¼in)
Length at front	47cm (18½in)	47cm (18½in)	47cm (18½in)	54cm (21¼in)	54cm (21¼in)	54cm (21¼in)	64cm (25¼in)	64cm (25¼in)	64cm (25¼in)	64cm (25¼in)
Length at back	54cm (21¼in)	54cm (21¼in)	54cm (21¼in)	61.5cm (24¼in)	61.5cm (24¼in)	61.5cm (24¼in)	71.5cm (28¼in)	71.5cm (28¼in)	71.5cm (28¼in)	71.5cm (28¼in)
Sleeve depth	15.5cm (6in)	16cm (6¼in)	18.5cm (7¼in)	20cm (8in)	20cm (8in)	22cm (8¾in)	24cm (9½in)	24cm (9½in)	25.5cm (10in)	27cm (10½in)

Pattern notes & chart

As your body panels are worked in turned rows there is no right
or wrong side, so just choose your favourite when seaming!

Chart shows pattern repeat for guidance on stitch placement within
the filet section only, place repeats within rows or rounds following
written instructions for your chosen size. Read even-number
rows from right to left and odd-number rows from left to right.

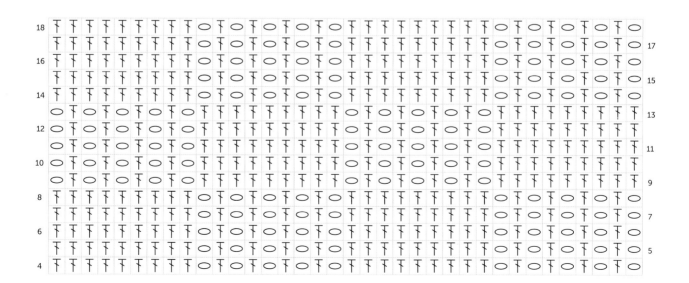

Back Panel

Row 1: Fdc55 (57, 65, 73) (77, 85, 91) (101, 105, 111), turn.

OR: Ch58 (60, 68, 76) (80, 88, 94) (104, 108, 114), 1dc in fourth ch from hook and each ch along, turn.

Row 2: Ch3 (does not count as a st throughout), 1dc in each st, turn.

Row 3: Rep Row 2.

Row 4: Ch3, 5 (6, 1, 5) (7, 2, 5) (1, 3, 6)dc, *[ch1, sk 1 st, 1dc] 4 times, ch1, sk 1 st, 9dc* 2 (2, 3, 3) (3, 4, 4) (5, 5, 5) times, [ch1, sk 1 st, 1dc] 4 times, ch1, sk 1 st, 5 (6, 1, 5) (7, 2, 5) (1, 3, 6)dc, turn.

Rows 5–8: Rep Row 4.

Sizes XXS (XS, M) (L, 2X) (5X) only:

Row 9: Ch3, 2 (1, 2) (2, 2) (1)dc, (ch1, sk 1 st, 1dc) 1 (2, 1) (2, 1) (2) times, ch1, sk 1 st, *9dc, [ch1, sk 1 st, 1dc] 4 times, ch1, sk 1 st* 2 (2, 3) (3, 4) (5) times, 9dc, [ch1, sk 1 st, 1dc] 1 (2, 1) (2, 1) (2) times, ch1, sk 1 st, 2 (1, 2) (2, 2) (1)dc, turn.

Rows 10–13: Rep Row 9.

Sizes (S) (XL) (3X, 4X):

Row 9: Ch3, (1) (2) (1, 3)dc, *9dc, [ch1, sk 1 st, 1dc] 4 times, ch1, sk 1 st* (3) (4) (5, 5) times, 9dc, (1) (2) (1, 3)dc, turn.

Rows 10–13: Rep Row 9.

All sizes:

Rep Rows 4–13 one (one, one, two) (two, two, two) (two, two, two) MORE times.

Sizes XXS (XS, S) (2X) (3X, 4X, 5X) only:

Rep Rows 4–8 once more.

All sizes:

There is now a total of 28 (28, 28, 33) (33, 33, 38) (38, 38, 38) rows.

Row 14: Ch3, 1dc in each st, turn.

Rep Row 14 nine (nine, nine, nine) (nine, nine, eleven) (eleven, eleven, eleven) MORE times for a total of 38 (38, 38, 43) (43, 43, 50) (50, 50, 50) rows.

Fasten off.

Front Panel

Row 1: Fdc55 (57, 65, 73) (77, 85, 91) (101, 105, 111), turn.

OR: Ch58 (60, 68, 76) (80, 88, 94) (104, 108, 114), 1dc in fourth ch from hook and each ch along, turn.

Row 2: Ch3 (does not count as a st throughout), 1dc in each st, turn.

Row 3: Rep row 2.

Sizes XXS (XS, M) (L, 2X) (5X) only:

Row 4: Ch3, 2 (1, 2) (2, 2) (1)dc, [ch1, sk 1 st, 1dc] 1 (2, 1) (2, 1) (2) times, ch1, sk 1 st, *9dc, [ch1, sk 1 st, 1dc] 4 times, ch1, sk 1 st* 2 (2, 3) (3, 4) (5) times, 9dc, [ch1, sk 1 st, 1dc] 1 (2, 1) (2, 1) (2) times, ch1, sk 1 st, 2 (1, 2) (2, 2) (2, 1)dc, turn.

Rows 5–8: Rep Row 4.

Sizes (S) (XL) (3X, 4X) only:

Row 4: Ch3, (1) (2) (1, 3)dc, *9dc, [ch1, sk 1 st, 1dc] 4 times, ch1, sk 1 st* (3) (4) (5, 5) times, 9dc, (1) (2) (1, 3)dc, turn.

Rows 5–8: Rep Row 4.

All sizes:

Row 9: Ch3, 5 (6, 1, 5) (7, 2, 5) (1, 3, 6)dc, *[ch1, sk 1 st, 1dc] 4 times, ch1, sk 1 st, 9dc* 2 (2, 3, 3) (3, 4, 4) (5, 5, 5) times, [ch1, sk 1 st, 1dc] 4 times, ch1, sk 1 st, 5 (6, 1, 5) (7, 2, 5) (1, 3, 6)dc, turn.

Rows 10–13: Rep Row 9.

Rep Rows 4–13 one (one, one, one) (one, one, two) (two, two, two) MORE times.

Sizes (M) (L, XL) only:

Rep Rows 4–8 once more.

All sizes:

There is now a total of 23 (23, 23, 28) (28, 28, 33) (33, 33, 33) rows.

Row 14: Ch3, 1dc in each st, turn.

Rep Row 14 six (five, five, five) (five, five, seven) (seven, seven, seven) MORE times for a total of 30 (29, 29, 34) (34, 34, 41) (41, 41, 41) rows.

Neckline one

Row 1: Ch3, 20 (21, 24, 28) (30, 34, 36) (41, 43, 46)dc, turn leaving rem sts unworked.

Row 2: Ch3, 1dc in each st, turn.

Row 3: Rep Row 2.

Size XXS only:

Move on to Row 5.

Sizes (XS, S, M) (L, XL, 2X) (3X, 4X, 5X) only:

Row 4: Ch3, 1dc in each st, turn.

All sizes:

Row 5: Ch1, with RS of Front and Back Panels tog, 1sc through next 20 (21, 24, 28) (30, 34, 36) (41, 43, 46) sts on both edges to seam shoulder.

Fasten off.

Neckline two

Count 20 (21, 24, 28) (30, 34, 36) (41, 43, 46) sts from other side of work, join yarn and rep Neckline One Rows 1–5.

Turtleneck

With RS facing join yarn in any st at back of neckline.

Round 1: Ch1, 1sc in each st along back of neckline, 2sc in each Neckline One row edge, 1sc in each st along front of neckline, 2sc in each Neckline Two row edge, 1sc in each st at back of neckline to ch-1, ss to join.

Row 2: Ch11, 1hdc in second ch from hook and each ch along, ss in next 2 sts from Row 1, turn.

Row 3: Sk 2 sts, 10hdcBLO, turn.

Row 4: Ch1, 10hdcBLO, ss in next 2 sts from Row 1, turn.

Rep Rows 3 and 4 around entire neckline, at start of turtleneck ss through both edges on WS to seam.

Fasten off.

> **TIP:** You can alter the width of your sleeve cuff by working more or fewer Row 2 repeats but be sure to work the same number of stitches evenly around in Round 3.

Sleeves
(make two)

Row 1: Fdc10, turn.

OR: Ch12, 1hdc in third ch from hook and each ch along, turn.

Row 2: Ch1 (does not count as a st throughout), 1hdcBLO in each st, turn.

Rep Row 2 until you have 16 (18, 19) (19, 19, 20) (20, 22, 23) rows.

At end of final row, turn, ch1, and seam cuff by working 1sc through each st on both edges to join, then turn RS out.

Round 3: Ch1, 2sc in each row edge around, ss to join, do not turn. 32 (36, 36, 38) (38, 38, 40) (40, 44, 46) sts

Sizes XXS (XS, S) (4X) only:

Round 4: Ch3 (does not count as a st throughout), 1dc, *3 (5, 2) (1) dc, 2dc in next st* to last 3 (5, 2) (1) st(s), 1dc in each rem st, ss to join, turn. 39 (41, 47) (65) sts

Sizes (M) (L, 2X) (3X, 5X) only:

Round 4: Ch3, 1dc, *(2) (2, 1) (1, 1) dc, 2dc in next st* to last st, (2) (2, 3) (3, 2)dc in last st, ss to join, turn. (51) (51, 61) (61, 69) sts

Size XL only:

Round 4: Ch3, 2dc, *1dc, 2dc in next st* to last 2 sts, 2dc, ss to join, turn. (55) sts

Sizes XXS (XS) (XL, 2X) (3X) only:

Round 5: Ch3, 7dc, *[ch1, sk 1 st, 1dc] 4 times, ch1, sk 1 st, 9dc* 1 (1) (2, 2) (2) times, [ch1, sk 1 st, 1dc] 4 times, ch1, sk 1 st, 5 (7) (3, 9) (9)dc, ss to join, turn.

Round 6: Ch3, 5 (7) (3, 9) (9)dc, *[ch1, sk 1 st, 1dc] 4 times, ch1, sk 1 st, 9dc* 1 (1) (2, 2) (2) times, [ch1, sk 1 st, 1dc] 4 times, ch1, sk 1 st, 7dc, ss to join, turn.

Round 7: Rep Round 5.

Round 8: Rep Round 6.

Round 9: Rep Round 5.

Round 10: Ch3, [ch1, sk 1 st, 1dc] 2 (3) (1, 4) (4) times, ch1, sk 1 st, *9dc, [ch1, sk 1 st, 1dc] 4 times, ch1, sk 1 st* 1 (1) (2, 2) (2) times, 9dc, [ch1, sk 1 st, 1dc] 3 times, ch1, sk 1 st, ss to join, turn.

Round 11: Ch3, [ch1, sk 1 st, 1dc] 3 times, ch1, sk 1 st, *9dc, [ch1, sk 1 st, 1dc] 4 times, ch1, sk 1 st* 1 (1) (2, 2) (2) times, 9dc, [ch1, sk 1 st, 1dc] 2 (3) (1, 4) (4) times, ch1, sk 1 st, ss to join, turn.

Round 12: Rep Round 10.

Round 13: Rep Round 11.

Round 14: Rep Round 10.

Rep Rounds 5–14 once more.

Sizes (S, M, L) (4X, 5X) only:

Round 5: Ch3, 7dc, *[ch1, sk 1 st, 1dc] 4 times, ch1, sk 1 st, 9dc* (2, 2) (2) (3, 3) times, [ch1, sk 1 st, 1dc] (2, 4) (4) (2, 4) times, ss to join, turn.

Round 6: Ch3, 1dc, [ch1, sk 1 st, 1dc] (1, 3) (3) (1, 3) times, ch1, sk 1 st, *9dc, [ch1, sk 1 st, 1dc] 4 times, ch1, sk 1 st* (2, 2) (2) (3, 3) times, 7dc, ss to join, turn.

Round 7: Rep Round 5.

Round 8: Rep Round 6.

Round 9: Rep Round 5.

Round 10: Ch3, (4, 8) (8) (4, 8) dc, *[ch1, sk 1 st, 1dc] 4 times, ch1, sk 1 st, 9dc* (2, 2) (2) (3, 3) times, [ch1, sk 1 st, 1dc] 3 times, ch1, sk 1 st, ss to join, turn.

Round 11: Ch3, [ch1, sk 1 st, 1dc] 3 times, ch1, sk 1 st, *9dc, [ch1, sk 1 st, 1dc] 4 times, ch1, sk 1 st* (2, 2) (2) (3, 3) times, (4, 8) (8) (4, 8)dc, ss to join, turn.

Round 12: Rep Round 10.

Round 13: Rep Round 11.

Round 14: Rep Round 10.

Rep Rounds 5–14 once more.

All sizes:

Round 15: Ch3, 1dc in each st, ss to join, turn.

Rep Round 15 four MORE times.

Fasten off.

Finishing

Lay body panels flat with WS facing. Lay Sleeve next to body panels and place marker where Sleeve join meets body. Align Front Panel Row 4 with Back Panel Row 9 and seam sides from here up to Sleeve marker, then join Sleeves to body panels.

Bottom edging

Join yarn in any st at back of work.

Round 1: Ch1, 1sc in each st around bottom edge of work to st before side split, 3sc in final st, 2sc in each row edge of split, ss in seam, 2sc in each row edge of split, 3sc in first st at bottom of Front Panel, 1sc along bottom edge. Rep as before for second split, then sc to ch-1, ss to join.

Fasten off and weave in all ends.

CLOUD= BUSTING VEST

Perfect for throwing over a T-shirt and shorts as an extra layer for spring dog walks, or pairing with a roll neck and jeans in the winter, the retro Cloudbusting Vest keeps the chill away without feeling bulky. The length of this is completely customisable but the yarn amounts are given for the length shown.

Gauge (tension)
13 sts x 7 rows = 10 x 10cm (4 x 4in) using 4mm (US size G/6) hook.

Yarn & hook
Paintbox Yarns Simply DK (100% acrylic), DK (light worsted) weight yarn, 276m (302yd) per 100g (3½oz) ball in the following shade:
• Slate Grey (105): 4¾ (4¾, 5¼, 5¾) (6, 6¾, 7) (7¾, 8½, 9) balls
4mm (US size G/6) crochet hook
2 stitch markers

	XXS	XS	S	M	L	XL	2X	3X	4X	5X
Circumference	90cm (35½in)	92.5cm (36½in)	107.5cm (42¼in)	119cm (46¾in)	125cm (49¼in)	136cm (53½in)	145cm (57in)	156cm (61½in)	165cm (65in)	177.5cm (70in)
Length	50cm (19¾in)	55cm (21¾in)	55cm (21¾in)	55cm (21¾in)	60cm (23½in)	60cm (23½in)	60cm (23½in)	65cm (25½in)	65cm (25½in)	65cm (25½in)

Pattern notes & chart

Chart shows pattern repeat for guidance on stitch placement within the filet section only, place repeats within rows or rounds following written instructions for your chosen size. Read RS (odd-number) rows from right to left and WS (even-number) rows from left to right.

Special abbreviation

Bead st (bead stitch): sk 1 st, 1dc, [yo, insert hook around post of dc just made, yo, pull back around stitch] 3 times, yo, pull through 5 loops on hook, yo, pull through 2 remaining loops

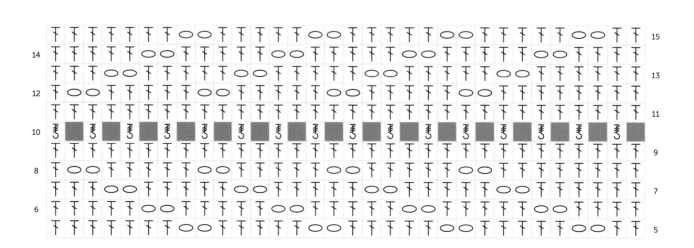

Back Panel

Row 1: Fdc72 (74, 86, 95) (100, 109, 116) (125, 132, 142), turn.

OR: Ch73 (75, 87, 96) (101, 110, 117) (126, 133, 143), 1dc in first ch from hook and each ch along, turn.

Row 2: Ch1 (does not count as a st throughout), 1dc in each st, turn.

Row 3 (RS): Ch1, 2dc, *sk next st, bead st in next st* to last 2 (2, 2, 3) (2, 3, 2) (3, 2, 2) sts, 1dc in each rem st, turn.

Row 4 (WS): Ch1, 1dc in each st, turn.

Row 5: Ch1, 1 (2, 1, 2) (1, 2, 2) (3, 3, 1)dc, *ch2, sk 2 sts, 5dc* to last 1 (2, 1, 2) (1, 2, 2) (3, 3, 1) sts, 1dc in each rem st, turn.

Row 6: Ch1, 4 (5, 4, 5) (4, 5, 5) (6, 6, 4)dc, *ch2, sk 2 sts, 5dc* to last 5 (6, 5, 6) (5, 6, 6) (7, 7, 5) sts, ch2, sk 2 sts, 3 (4, 3, 4) (3, 4, 4) (5, 5, 3)dc, turn.

Row 7: Ch1, 5 (6, 5, 6) (5, 6, 6) (7, 7, 5)dc, *ch2, sk 2 sts, 5dc* to last 4 (5, 4, 5) (4, 5, 5) (6, 6, 4) sts, ch2, sk 2 sts, 2 (3, 2, 3) (2, 3, 3) (4, 4, 2)dc, turn.

Row 8: Ch1, 7 (8, 7, 8) (7, 8, 8) (9, 9, 7)dc, *ch2, sk 2 sts, 5dc* to last 2 (3, 2, 3) (2, 3, 3) (4, 4, 2) sts, 1dc in each rem st, turn.

Row 9: Ch1, 1dc in each st, turn.

Row 10: Ch1, 2dc, *sk next st, bead st in next st* to last 2 (2, 2, 3) (2, 3, 2) (3, 2, 2) sts, 1dc in each rem st, turn.

Row 11: Ch1, 1dc in each st, turn.

Row 12: Rep Row 8.

Row 13: Rep Row 7.

Row 14: Rep Row 6.

Row 15: Rep Row 5.

Rep Rows 2–15 until Back Panel is desired length, ending on a Row 4 or 11 rep, then rep Row 2 once more.

Fasten off.

TIP: This pattern uses a turning ch1 to keep the edges straight – this does not count as a stitch throughout.

Front Panels

(make two)

Row 1: Fdc34 (34, 44, 46) (48, 55, 58) (62, 67, 72), turn.

OR: Ch35 (35, 45, 47) (49, 56, 59) (63, 68, 73), 1dc in first ch from hook and each ch along, turn.

Row 2: Ch1 (does not count as a st throughout), 1dc in each st, turn.

Row 3 (RS): Ch1, 2dc, *sk next st, bead st in next st* to last 2 (2, 2, 2) (2, 3, 2) (2, 3, 2) sts, 1dc in each rem st, turn.

Row 4 (WS): Ch1, 1dc in each st, turn.

Row 5: Ch1, 3 (3, 1, 2) (3, 3, 1) (3, 2, 1)dc, *ch2, sk 2 sts, 5dc* to last 3 (3, 1, 2) (3, 3, 1) (3, 2, 1) sts, 1dc in each rem st, turn.

Row 6: Ch1, 6 (6, 4, 5) (6, 6, 4) (6, 5, 4)dc, *ch2, sk 2 sts, 5dc* to last 7 (7, 5, 6) (7, 7, 5) (7, 6, 5) sts, 1dc in each rem st, turn.

Row 7: Ch1, 7 (7, 5, 6) (7, 7, 5) (7, 6, 5)dc, *ch2, sk 2 sts, 5dc* to last 6 (6, 4, 5) (6, 6, 4) (6, 5, 4) sts, ch2, sk 2 sts, 1dc in each rem st, turn.

Row 8: Ch1, 9 (9, 7, 8) (9, 9, 7) (9, 8, 7)dc, *5dc, ch2, sk 2 sts* to last 4 (4, 2, 3) (4, 4, 2) (4, 3, 2) sts, 1dc in each rem st, turn.

Row 9: Ch1, 1dc in each st, turn.

Row 10: Ch1, 2dc, *sk next st, bead st in next st* to last 2 (2, 2, 2) (2, 3, 2) (2, 3, 2) sts, 1dc in each rem st, turn.

Row 11: Ch1, 1dc in each st, turn.

Row 12: Ch1, 9 (9, 7, 8) (9, 9, 7) (9, 8, 7)dc, *5dc, ch2, sk 2 sts* to last 4 (4, 2, 3) (4, 4, 2) (4, 3, 2) sts, 1dc in each rem st, turn.

Row 13: Ch1, 7 (7, 5, 6) (7, 7, 5) (7, 6, 5)dc, *ch2, sk 2 sts, 5dc* to last 6 (6, 4, 5) (6, 6, 4) (6, 5, 4) sts, ch2, sk 2 sts, 1dc in each rem st, turn.

Row 14: Ch1, 6 (6, 4, 5) (6, 6, 4) (6, 5, 4)dc, *ch2, sk 2 sts, 5dc* to last 7 (7, 5, 6) (7, 7, 5) (7, 6, 5) sts, ch2, sk 2 sts, 1dc in each rem st, turn.

Row 15: Ch1, 3 (3, 1, 2) (3, 3, 1) (3, 2, 1)dc, *ch2, sk 2 sts, 5dc* to last 3 (3, 1, 2) (3, 3, 1) (3, 2, 1) sts, 1dc in each rem st, turn.

Rep Rows 2–15 until Front Panel is same length as Back Panel, remembering to rep Row 2 one final time.

Fasten off.

Shoulder seaming

With RS of Back and Front Panels tog, seam shoulders from outer edge inwards, leaving 19 (20, 22, 21) (21, 22, 23) (23, 25, 25) sts open at inner end of each Front Panel.

Hood

With RS facing, join yarn at front left of neckline.

Row 1 (RS): Ch1, 1dc in each st around entire neckline.

Sizes XXS, (M) (XL, 2X) only:

Work 2dc in one st at back of neckline to inc st count by one st.

Sizes (4X, 5X) only:

Work 2dc into each of two sts at back of neckline to inc st count by two sts.

All sizes:

There are now 81 (86, 86, 88) (88, 88, 93) (93, 100, 100) sts.

Row 2 (WS): Ch1, 2dc, *sk next st, bead st in next st* to last 3 (2, 2, 2) (2, 2, 3) (3, 2, 2) sts, 1dc in each rem st, turn.

Row 3: Ch1, 1dc in each st, turn.

Row 4: Ch1, 2 (1, 1, 2) (2, 2, 1) (1, 1, 1)dc, *ch2, sk 2 sts, 5dc* to last 2 (1, 1, 2) (2, 2, 1) (1, 1, 1) sts, 1dc in each rem st, turn.

Row 5: Ch1, 5 (4, 4, 5) (5, 5, 4) (4, 4, 4)dc, *ch2, sk 2 sts, 5dc* to last 6 (5, 5, 6) (6, 6, 5) (5, 5, 5) sts, ch2, sk 2 sts, 1dc in each rem st, turn.

Row 6: Ch1, 6 (5, 5, 6) (6, 6, 5) (5, 5, 5)dc, *ch2, sk 2 sts, 5dc* to last 5 (4, 4, 5) (5, 5, 4) (4, 4, 4) sts, ch2, sk 2 sts, 1dc in each rem st, turn.

Row 7: Ch1, 8 (7, 7, 8) (8, 8, 7) (7, 7, 7)dc, *ch2, sk 2 sts, 5dc* to last 3 (2, 2, 3) (3, 3, 2) (2, 2, 2) sts, 1dc in each rem st, turn.

Row 8: Ch1, 1dc in each st, turn.

Row 9: Ch1, 2dc, *sk next st, bead st in next st* to last 3 (2, 2, 2) (2, 2, 3) (3, 2, 2) sts, 1dc in each rem st, turn.

Row 10: Ch1, 1dc in each st, turn.

Row 11: Rep Row 7.

Row 12: Rep Row 6.

Row 13: Rep Row 5.

Row 14: Rep Row 4.

Round 15: Ch3, 1dc in each st, turn.

Rep Rows 2–15 twice more.

Hood seaming

With RS tog, ch1 and sc through each st on either edge to seam top of Hood.

Fasten off.

Pockets

(make two)

Work as per Front Panel until end of Row 15, then rep Row 2 once more.

Final row: Ch1, 1sc in each st.

Fasten off, leaving a long tail for seaming.

Belt

Row 1: Fdc12, turn.

OR: Ch15, 1dc in fourth ch from hook and each ch along, turn.

Row 2: Ch1, 2dc, [sk next st, bead st in next st] to last 2 sts, 2dc, turn.

Row 3: Ch1, 1dc in each st, turn.

Row 4: Ch1, [1sc, 1dc] to end, turn.

Rep Row 4 until Belt is desired length.

NOTE: Make sure you allow enough length to tie the belt in a jazzy bow if your heart desires.

Row 5: Ch1, 1dc in each st, turn.

Row 6: Rep Row 2.

Row 7: Ch1, 1dc in each st.

Fasten off.

Belt Loops

(make two)

Row 1: Leaving a long tail, fdc14.

OR: Ch15, 1dc in first ch from hook and each ch along.

Fasten off, leaving a long tail for seaming.

Finishing

Try vest on and place a marker where bottom of armhole is to sit. With RS of Back and Front Panels tog, seam up to marker on each side, then turn work RS out.

Sew Pockets to Front Panels using yarn tail, making sure pattern matches panel beneath.

Sew Belt Loops to edge of vest by side seam, using yarn tail.

Armhole edging

Join yarn in either st by seam at base of armhole.

Round 1: Ch1, work 2sc through each row end around armhole edge, ss in ch-1 to join.

Fasten off.

Front edging

With RS facing join yarn at hem of left Front Panel.

Row 1: Ch1, 2sc through each row end of left Front Panel up to Hood, being sure to work through Pocket edge for a neat finish, 1sc in each st around Hood edge, 2sc through each row end on right Front Panel.

Fasten off.

ONLY YOU TOP

A sweet and subtle nod to filet, the heart-shaped hemline of the Only You Top makes this is a super-cute addition to any outfit. Make it in pastel tones for a classically pretty piece, or in deep jewel colours for a grown up twist. Whichever colour you choose, you'll be feeling the love in this simple make.

Gauge (tension)

16 sts x 9 rows = 10 x 10cm (4 x 4in) using 4mm (US size G/6) hook.

Yarn & hook

Paintbox Yarns Simply DK (100% acrylic), DK (light worsted) weight yarn, 276m (302yd) per 100g (3½oz) ball in the following shade:
• Jewel (72): 2¼ (3, 3, 3½) (3¾, 4, 5) (5¼, 5½, 6) balls

4mm (US size G/6) crochet hook

2 stitch markers

	XXS	XS	S	M	L	XL	2X	3X	4X	5X
Circumference	67.5cm (26½in)	77.5cm (30½in)	87.5cm (34½in)	97.5cm (38½in)	107.5cm (42¼in)	117.5cm (46¼in)	127.5cm (50¼in)	137.5cm (54in)	147.5cm (58in)	157.5cm (62in)
Length	46.5cm (18¼in)	46.5cm (18¼in)	46.5cm (18¼in)	46.5cm (18¼in)	46.5cm (18¼in)	53cm (21in)	53cm (21in)	60cm (23½in)	60cm (23½in)	60cm (23½in)
Sleeve depth	15.5cm (6in)	17cm (6¾in)	17cm (6¾in)	19cm (7½in)	20.5cm (8in)	23cm (9in)	23cm (9in)	24.5cm (9¾in)	26cm (10¼in)	26cm (10¼in)

Pattern notes & chart

Be sure to work your chains in the filet section really loosely to ensure the heart design doesn't pucker.

Chart shows pattern repeat for guidance on stitch placement within the filet section only, place repeats within rows or rounds following written instructions for your chosen size. Read RS (odd-number) rows from right to left and WS (even-number) rows from left to right.

Special abbreviation

Crossed dc (crossed double crochet): sk 1 st, 1dc in next st, then working in front of st just made, 1dc in skipped st

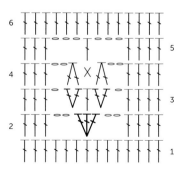

Back Panel

Row 1: Fdc54 (62, 70, 78) (86, 94, 102) (110, 118, 126), turn.

OR: Ch57 (65, 73, 81) (89, 97, 105) (113, 121, 129), 1dc in fourth ch from hook and each ch along, turn.

Row 2 (WS): Ch3 (does not count as a st throughout), 4dc, *ch2, sk 3 sts, 3dc in next st, ch2, sk 3 sts, 1dc* to last 2 sts, 2dc, turn.

NOTE: Your chain here is meant to be one shorter than the number of skipped stitches, that's not a mistake!

Row 3 (RS): Ch3, 3dc, *ch1, sk 2 ch, 2dc in next st, 1dc, 2dc in next st, ch1, sk 2 ch, 1dc* to last 3 sts, 1dc in each rem st, turn.

Row 4: Ch3, 4dc, *ch2, sk 1 ch, dc2tog, 1sc, dc2tog, ch2, sk 1 ch, 1dc* to last 2 sts, 2dc, turn.

Row 5: Ch3, 3dc, *ch3, sk 2 ch and 1 st, 1dc, ch3, sk 1 st and 2 ch, 1dc* to last 3 sts, 3dc, turn.

Row 6: Ch3, 4dc, *3dc in ch-3 sp, 1dc, 3dc in ch-3 sp, 1dc* to last 2 sts, 2dc, turn.

Row 7: Ch3, 2dc, *crossed dc over next 2 sts* to last 2 sts, 2dc, turn.

Rows 8–12: Ch3, 1dc in each st, turn.

Rep Rows 7–12 five (five, five, five) (five, six, six) (seven, seven, seven) MORE times for a total of 42 (42, 42, 42) (42, 48, 48) (54, 54, 54) rows.

Fasten off.

Front Panel

Work as per Back Panel to four rows short of Back Panel length, then work Neckline One.

Neckline one

Row 1: Ch3, 12 (16, 20, 24) (28, 32, 36) (40, 44, 48)dc, turn.

Row 2: Ch3, 1dc in each st, turn.

Rows 3 and 4: Rep Row 2.

Row 5: Ch1, with RS of Front and Back Panels tog, 1sc through next 12 (16, 20, 24) (28, 32, 36) (40, 44, 48) sts on both edges to join shoulder.

Fasten off.

Neckline two

Count 12 (16, 20, 24) (28, 32, 36) (40, 44, 48) sts from other edge of work and join yarn.

Row 1: Ch3, 12 (16, 20, 24) (28, 32, 36) (40, 44, 48)dc, turn.

Row 2: Ch3, 1dc in each st, turn.

Rows 3 and 4: Rep Row 2.

Row 5: Ch1, with RS of Front and Back Panels tog, 1sc through next 12 (16, 20, 24) (28, 32, 36) (40, 44, 48) sts on both edges to join shoulder.

Fasten off.

Neckline edging

With RS facing, join yarn in central st at back of neckline.

Round 1: Ch1, 1sc loosely in each st along back of neckline, 2sc in each row end of Neckline One, 1sc in each st along front of neckline, 2sc in each row end of Neckline Two, 1sc in each rem st at back of neckline, ss in ch-1 to join.

Round 2: Ch1, 1sc, *sk 2 sts, 5dc in next st, sk 2 sts, 1sc* around, ss in ch-1 to join.

Fasten off.

NOTE: You may want to size up your hook to make sure your neckline doesn't end up too tight. You can omit Round 2 for a plain neckline.

Sleeves

(make two)

Row 1: Fdc50 (54, 54, 60) (60, 60, 60) (60, 60, 60), turn.

OR: Ch53 (57, 57, 63) (63, 63, 63) (63, 63, 63), 1dc in fourth ch from hook and each ch along, turn.

Row 2 (WS): Ch3 (does not count as a st throughout), 2 (4, 4, 3) (3, 3, 3) (3, 3, 3)dc, *ch2, sk 3 sts, 3dc in next st, ch2, sk 3 sts, 1dc* to last 0 (2, 2, 1) (1, 1, 1) (1, 1, 1) sts, 1dc in each rem st, turn.

Row 3 (RS): Ch3, 1 (3, 3, 2) (2, 2, 2) (2, 2, 2)dc, *ch1, sk 2 ch, 2dc in next st, 1dc, 2dc in next st, ch1, sk 2 ch, 1dc* to last 1 (3, 3, 2) (2, 2, 2) (2, 2, 2) sts, 1dc in each rem st, turn.

Row 4: Ch3, 2 (4, 4, 3) (3, 3, 3) (3, 3, 3)dc, *ch2, sk 1 ch, dc2tog, 1sc, dc2tog, ch2, sk 1 ch, 1dc* to last 0 (2, 2, 1) (1, 1, 1) (1, 1, 1) sts, 1dc in each rem st, turn.

Row 5: Ch3, 1 (3, 3, 2) (2, 2, 2) (2, 2, 2)dc, *ch3, sk 2 ch and 1 st, 1dc, ch3, sk 1 st and 2 ch, 1dc* to last 1 (3, 3, 2) (2, 2, 2) (2, 2, 2) sts, 1dc in each rem st, turn.

Row 6: Ch3, 2 (4, 4, 3) (3, 3, 3) (3, 3, 3)dc, *3dc in 3ch-sp, 1dc, 3dc in 3ch-sp, 1dc* to last 0 (2, 2, 1) (1, 1, 1) (1, 1, 1) sts, 1dc in each rem st, turn.

Sizes XXS (XS, S, M) only:

Move on to Straight Sleeve Rows.

Sizes (L, XL, 2X) (3X, 4X, 5X) only:

Sleeve increase rows

Row 1: Ch3, 2dc, *crossed dc over next 2 sts* to last 2 sts, 2dc, turn.

Row 2: Ch3, 2dc in first st, 1dc in each rem st, turn. (61, 61, 61) (61, 61, 61) sts

Rows 3–6: Rep Row 2. (65, 65, 65) (65, 65, 65) sts

Row 7: Ch3, 2dc in first st, 1dc in same st as first st to create first crossed dc and inc, *crossed dc over next 2 sts* to last 2 sts, 2dc, turn. (66, 66, 66) (66, 66, 66) sts

Size (L) only:

Move on to Straight Sleeve Rows.

Sizes (XL, 2X) (3X, 4X, 5X) only:

Rows 8–13: Rep Rows 2–7. (72, 72) (72, 72, 72) sts

Rows 14 and 15: Rep Rows 2 and 3. (74, 74) (74, 74, 74) sts

Sizes (XL, 2X) only:

Move on to Straight Sleeve Rows.

Sizes (3X, 4X, 5X) only:

Rows 16–19: Rep Rows 4–7. (78, 78, 78) sts

Size (3X) only:

Move on to Straight Sleeve Rows.

Sizes (4X, 5X) only:

Rows 20–25: Rep Rows 2–7. (84, 84) sts

Move on to Straight Sleeve Rows.

Straight sleeve rows

Start on Row 1 (1, 1, 1) (2, 4, 4) (2, 2, 2).

Row 1: Ch3, 2dc, *crossed dc over next 2 sts* to last 2 sts, 2dc, turn.

Rows 2–6: Ch3, 1dc in each st, turn. 50 (54, 54, 60) (66, 74, 74) (78, 84, 84) sts

Rep Rows 1–6 until Sleeve sits at elbow, approx. 30 rows in total. Do not fasten off.

Finishing

Sleeve seam and edging

Seaming row: Ch1, fold Sleeve in half lengthways with RS tog, 2sc through each row end on both sides to Sleeve Row 1 to seam Sleeve, turn RS out.

Round 1: Ch1, with RS facing 1sc loosely in each st around Sleeve edge, ss in ch-1 to join, do not turn.

Sizes (XL, 2X) only:

Work 2 sc2tog spaced evenly apart to bring total st count to 72 sts.

All sizes:

Round 2: Ch1, *sk 2 sts, 5dc in next st, sk 2 sts, 1sc* around Sleeve edge, ss in ch-1 to join.

Fasten off.

Seaming

Lay body panels flat with WS facing. Lay Sleeve next to body panels and place marker where Sleeve join meets body. Find Front Panel Row 7 and place marker through to join with Row 7 on Back Panel. Seam sides from here up to Sleeve marker, then join Sleeves to body panels.

Bottom edging

With RS facing join yarn in first st at left-hand side of Front Panel.

Round 1: Ch1, [1sc in each st along bottom edge of Front Panel to side split, 2sc in each row end around side split] twice, ss in ch-1 to join.

Round 2: **Ch1, 3 (1, 2, 3) (1, 2, 3) (1, 2, 3) sc, *sk 2 sts, 5dc in next st, sk 2 sts, 1sc* to last 3 (1, 2, 3) (1, 2, 3) (1, 2, 3) sts before side split, 3 (1, 2, 3) (1, 2, 3) (1, 2, 3) sc, 1sc in each side split st; rep from ** along Back Panel, ss in ch-1 to join.

Fasten off, and weave in all ends.

HONEY TO THE BEE SWEATER

Unbelievably snug and amazingly eye-catching, you won't bee-lieve how easily this sweater works up. Once you're in the flow of the repetitive stitch pattern you'll barely have to think about it, but it gives the most beautiful result. The roll neck is perfect for the cooler months, making this cosy aran sweater a firm favourite.

Gauge (tension)

13 sts x 7 rows = 10 x 10cm (4 x 4in) using 5mm (US size H/8) hook.

Yarn & hook

Paintbox Yarns Simply Aran (100% acrylic), aran (worsted) weight yarn, 184m (201yd) per 100g (3½oz) ball in the following shade:
• Light Caramel (208): 5 (6, 6½, 6¾) (7¾, 8¼, 9¼) (10, 10¼, 11) balls
5mm (US size H/8) crochet hook

	XXS	XS	S	M	L	XL	2X	3X	4X	5X
Circumference	81.5cm (32in)	91cm (35¾in)	100cm (39¼in)	109cm (43in)	118.5cm (46¾in)	134cm (52¾in)	140cm (55in)	152cm (59¾in)	159cm (62½in)	171cm (67¼in)
Length	51cm (20in)	57cm (22½in)	57cm (22½in)	57cm (22½in)	62.5cm (24½in)	62.5cm (24½in)	68cm (26¾in)	68cm (26¾in)	68cm (26¾in)	68cm (26¾in)
Sleeve depth	17.5cm (7in)	17.5cm (7in)	17.5cm (7in)	19cm (7½in)	19cm (7½in)	22cm (8¾in)	22cm (8¾in)	25cm (9¾in)	25cm (9¾in)	29.5cm (11½in)

Pattern notes & chart

As your body panels are worked in turned rows there is no right or wrong side, so just choose your favourite when seaming! If you would prefer a simple ribbed neckline instead of a cowl, only work the neckline rows on one panel, working plain double crochet in their place for the other.

Chart shows pattern repeat for guidance on stitch placement within the filet section only, place repeats within rows or rounds following written instructions for your chosen size. Read odd-number rows from right to left and even-number rows from left to right.

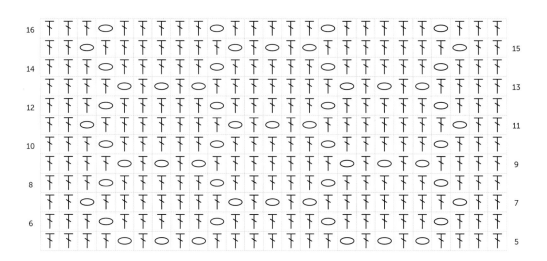

Body Panels

(make two)

Row 1: Fdc53 (59, 65, 71) (77, 87, 91) (99, 103, 111), turn.

OR: Ch56 (62, 68, 74) (80, 90, 94) (102, 105, 114), 1dc in fourth ch from hook and each ch along, turn.

Row 2: Ch3 (does not count as a st throughout), 1dc in each st, turn.

Row 3: Rep Row 2.

Size XXS only:

Move on to Honeycomb Section One.

All other sizes:

Row 4: Rep Row 2.

Honeycomb section one

Row 5: Ch3, 6 (3, 6, 3) (6, 5, 7) (5, 7, 5)dc, *[ch1, sk 1 st, 1dc] twice, ch1, sk 1 st, 7dc* 3 (4, 4, 5) (5, 6, 6) (7, 7, 8) times, [ch1, sk 1 st, 1dc] twice, ch1, sk 1 st, 6 (3, 6, 3) (6, 5, 7) (5, 7, 5)dc, turn.

Row 6: Ch3, 5 (2, 5, 2) (5, 4, 6) (4, 6, 4)dc, *ch1, sk 1 st, 5dc* 7 (9, 9, 11) (11, 13, 13) (15, 15, 17) times, ch1, sk 1 st, 5 (2, 5, 2) (5, 4, 6) (4, 6, 4)dc, turn.

Row 7: Ch3, 4 (1, 4, 1) (4, 3, 5) (3, 5, 3)dc, *ch1, sk 1 st, 7dc, [ch1, sk 1 st, 1dc] twice* 3 (4, 4, 5) (5, 6, 6) (7, 7, 8) times, ch1, sk 1 st, 7dc, ch1, sk 1 st, 4 (1, 4, 1) (4, 3, 5) (3, 5, 3)dc, turn.

Row 8: Rep Row 6.

Rep Rows 5–8 five (five, five, four) (five, five, six) (five, five, five) MORE times for a total of 27 (28, 28, 24) (28, 28, 32) (28, 28, 28) rows.

Honeycomb section two

Sizes XXS (M) (L) (3X, 4X) only:

Row 9: Rep Row 5.

Row 10: Ch3, 5 (2) (5) (4, 6)dc, *ch1, sk 1 st, 5dc* 2 (4) (4) (6, 6) times, ch1, sk 1 st, 17dc, *ch1, sk 1 st, 5dc* 2 (4) (4) (6, 6) times, ch1, sk 1 st, 5 (2) (5) (4, 6)dc, turn.

Row 11: Ch3, 4 (1) (4) (3, 5)dc, *ch1, sk 1 st, 7dc, [ch1, sk 1 st, 1dc] twice* 1 (2) (2) (3, 3) times, ch1, sk 1 st, 19dc, *[ch1, sk 1 st, 1dc] twice, ch1, sk 1 st, 7dc* 1 (2) (2) (3, 3) times, ch1, sk 1 st, 4 (1) (4) (3, 5)dc, turn.

Row 12: Ch3, 5 (2) (5) (4, 6)dc, *ch1, sk 1 st, 5dc* 1 (3) (3) (5, 5) times, ch1, sk 1 st, 29dc, *ch1, sk 1 st, 5dc* 1 (3) (3) (5, 5) times, ch1, sk 1 st, 5 (2) (5) (4, 6)dc, turn.

Size XXS only:

Row 13: Ch3, 6dc, [ch1, sk 1 st, 1dc] twice, ch1, sk 1 st, 31dc, [ch1, sk 1 st, 1dc] twice, ch1, sk 1 st, 6dc, turn.

Move on to Upper Body.

Sizes (M) (L) (3X, 4X) only:

Row 13: Ch3, (3) (6) (5, 7)dc, *[ch1, sk 1 st, 1dc] twice, ch1, sk 1 st, 7dc* (2) (2) (3, 3) times, 24dc, *[ch1, sk 1 st, 1dc] twice, ch1, sk 1 st, 7dc* (1) (1) (2, 2) times, [ch1, sk 1 st, 1dc] twice, ch1, sk 1 st, (3) (6) (5, 7)dc, turn.

Row 14: Ch3, (2) (5) (4, 6)dc, *ch1, sk 1 st, 5dc* (2) (2) (4, 4) times, ch1, sk 1 st, 41dc, *ch1, sk 1 st, 5dc* (2) (2) (4, 4) times, ch1, sk 1 st, (2) (5) (4, 6)dc, turn.

Row 15: Ch3, (1) (4) (3, 5)dc, *ch1, sk 1 st, 7dc, [ch1, sk 1 st, 1dc] twice* (1) (1) (2, 2) times, ch1, sk 1 st, 43dc, *[ch1, sk 1 st, 1dc] twice, ch1, sk 1 st, 7dc* (1) (1) (2, 2) times, ch1, sk 1 st, (1) (4) (3, 5)dc, turn.

Row 16: Ch3, (2) (5) (4, 6)dc, *ch1, sk 1 st, 5dc* (1) (1) (3, 3) times, ch1, sk 1 st, 53dc, *ch1, sk 1 st, 5dc* (1) (1) (3, 3) times, ch1, sk 1 st, (2) (5) (4, 6)dc, turn.

Sizes (M) (L) only:

Row 17: Ch3, (3) (6)dc, [ch1, sk 1 st, 1dc] twice, ch1, sk 1 st, 55dc, [ch1, sk 1 st, 1dc] twice, ch1, sk 1 st, (3) (6)dc, turn.

Move on to Upper Body.

Sizes (3X, 4X) only:

Row 17: Ch3, (5, 7)dc, *[ch1, sk 1 st, 1dc] twice, ch1, sk 1 st, 7dc* twice, 48dc, [ch1, sk 1 st, 1dc] twice, ch1, sk 1 st, 7dc, [ch1, sk 1 st, 1dc] twice, ch1, sk 1 st, (5, 7)dc, turn.

Row 18: Ch3, (4, 6)dc, *ch1, sk 1 st, 5dc* twice, ch1, sk 1 st, 65dc, *ch1, sk 1 st, 5dc* twice, ch1, sk 1 st, (4, 6)dc, turn.

Row 19: Ch3, (3, 5) dc, ch1, sk 1 st, 7dc, [ch1, sk 1 st, 1dc] twice, ch1, sk 1 st, 67dc, [ch1, sk 1 st, 1dc] twice, ch1, sk 1 st, 7dc, ch1, sk 1 st, (3, 5)dc, turn.

Row 20: Ch3, (4, 6)dc, ch1, sk 1 st, 5dc, ch1, sk 1 st, 77dc, ch1, sk 1 st, 5dc, ch1, sk 1 st, (4, 6)dc, turn.

Row 21: Ch3, (5, 7)dc, [ch1, sk 1 st, 1dc] twice, ch1, sk 1 st, 79dc, [ch1, sk 1 st, 1dc] twice, ch1, sk 1 st, (5, 7)dc, turn.

Move on to Upper Body.

Sizes (XS, S) (XL, 2X) (5X) only:

Row 9: Rep Row 5.

Row 10: Ch3, (2, 5) (4, 6) (4)dc, *ch1, sk 1 st, 5dc* (2, 2) (4, 4) (6) times, ch1, sk 1 st, 29dc, *ch1, sk 1 st, 5dc* (2, 2) (4, 4) (6) times, ch1, sk 1 st, (2, 5) (4, 6) (4)dc, turn.

Row 11: Ch3, (1, 4) (3, 5) (3)dc, *ch1, sk 1 st, 7dc, [ch1, sk 1 st, 1dc] twice* (1, 1) (2, 2) (3) times, ch1, sk 1 st, 31dc, *[ch1, sk 1 st, 1dc] twice, ch1, sk 1 st, 7dc* (1, 1) (2, 2) (3) times, ch1, sk 1 st, (1, 4) (3, 5) (3)dc, turn.

Row 12: Ch3, (2, 5) (4, 6) (4)dc, *ch1, sk 1 st, 5dc* (1, 1) (3, 3) (5) times, ch1, sk 1 st, 41dc, *ch1, sk 1 st, 5dc* (1, 1) (3, 3) (5) times, ch1, sk 1 st, (2, 5) (4, 6) (4)dc, turn.

Sizes (XS, S) only:

Row 13: Ch3, (3, 6)dc, [ch1, sk 1 st, 1dc] twice, ch1, sk 1 st, 43dc, [ch1, sk 1 st, 1dc] twice, ch1, sk 1 st, (3, 6)dc, turn.

Move on to Upper Body.

Sizes (XL, 2X) (5X) only:

Row 13: Ch3, (5, 7) (5)dc, *[ch1, sk 1 st, 1dc] twice, ch1, sk 1 st, 7dc* (2, 2) (3) times, 36dc, *[ch1, sk 1 st, 1dc] twice, ch1, sk 1 st, 7dc* (1, 1) (2) times, (ch1, sk 1 st, 1dc) twice, ch1, sk 1 st, (5, 7) (5)dc, turn.

Row 14: Ch3, (4, 6) (4)dc, *ch1, sk 1 st, 5dc* (2, 2) (4) times, ch1, sk 1 st, 53dc, *ch1, sk 1 st, 5dc* (2, 2) (4) times, ch1, sk 1 st, (4, 6) (4)dc, turn.

Row 15: Ch3, (3, 5) (3)dc, *ch1, sk 1 st, 7dc, [ch1, sk 1 st, 1dc] twice* (1, 1) (2) times, ch1, sk 1 st, 55dc, *[ch1, sk 1 st, 1dc] twice, ch1, sk 1 st, 7dc* (1, 1) (2) times, ch1, sk 1 st, (3, 5) (3)dc, turn.

Row 16: Ch3, (4, 6) (4)dc, *ch1, sk 1 st, 5dc* (1, 1) (3) times, ch1, sk 1 st, 65dc, *ch1, sk 1 st, 5dc* (1, 1) (3) times, ch1, sk 1 st, (4, 6) (4)dc, turn.

Sizes (XL, 2X) only:

Row 17: Ch3, (5, 7)dc, [ch1, sk 1 st, 1dc] twice, ch1, sk 1 st, 67dc, [ch1, sk 1 st, 1dc] twice, ch1, sk 1 st, (5, 7)dc, turn.

Move on to Upper Body.

Size 5X only:

Row 17: Ch3, 5dc, [ch1, sk 1 st, 1dc] twice, ch1, sk 1 st, 7dc, [ch1, sk 1 st, 1dc] twice, ch1, sk 1 st, 67dc, [ch1, sk 1 st, 1dc] twice, ch1, sk 1 st, 7dc, [ch1, sk 1 st, 1dc] twice, ch1, sk 1 st, 5dc, turn.

Row 18: Ch3, 4dc, *ch1, sk 1 st, 5dc* twice, ch1, sk 1 st, 77dc, *ch1, sk 1 st, 5dc* twice, ch1, sk 1 st, 4dc, turn.

Row 19: Ch3, 3dc, ch1, sk 1 st, 7dc, [ch1, sk 1 st, 1dc] twice, ch1, sk 1 st, 79dc, [ch1, sk 1 st, 1dc] twice, ch1, sk 1 st, 7dc, ch1, sk 1 st, 3dc, turn.

Row 20: Ch3, 4dc, ch1, sk 1 st, 5dc, ch1, sk 1 st, 89dc, ch1, sk 1 st, 5dc, ch1, sk 1 st, 4dc, turn.

Row 21: Ch3, 5dc, [ch1, sk 1 st, 1dc] twice, ch1, sk 1 st, 91dc, [ch1, sk 1 st, 1dc] twice, ch1, sk 1 st, 5dc, turn.

Move on to Upper Body.

Upper body

Row 1: Ch3, 1dc in each st, turn. 53 (59, 65, 71) (77, 87, 91) (99, 103, 111) sts

Size XXS only:

Move on to Neckline One.

All other sizes:

Row 2: Rep Row 1.

Row 3: Rep Row 1.

Move on to Neckline One.

Neckline one

Row 1: Ch3, 18 (18, 22, 25) (28, 33, 35) (38, 40, 43)dc, turn.

Row 2: Ch3, 1dc in each st, turn.

Row 3: Ch3, 1dc in each st, turn.

Size XXS only:

Fasten off here on first panel and work Neckline Two, work Row 5 on second panel.

All other sizes:

Row 4: Ch3, 1dc in each st, turn.

Fasten off here on first panel and work Neckline Two, work Row 5 on second panel.

All sizes second panel only:

Row 5: Ch1, with RS of both panels tog, 1sc through next 18 (18, 22, 25) (28, 33, 35) (38, 40, 43) sts on both edges to seam shoulder.

Fasten off.

Neckline two

Count 18 (18, 22, 25) (28, 33, 35) (38, 40, 43) sts from other edge of piece and join yarn, then rep Neckline One.

Roll neck

With RS facing join your yarn in any st at the back of your neckline.

Row 1: Ch1, 1sc in each st along back of neckline, 2sc in each neckline row edge on both panels, 1sc in each st along front neckline, 2sc in each neckline row edge as before, 1sc in each rem st at back of neckline, ss in ch-1 to join.

Row 2: Ch41, 1sc in second ch from hook and each ch along, then ss in next 2 sts from Row 1, turn.

NOTE: This creates a deep cowl, for a shorter roll neck work a shorter chain here.

Row 3: Sk 2 sts, 40scBLO, turn.

Row 4: Ch1, 40scBLO, ss in next 2 sts from Row 1, turn.

NOTE: For a looser roll neck, ss in next stitch from Row 1 and turn rather than in next 2 stitches.

Rep Rows 3 and 4 around neckline, at start of cowl ss through both edges on WS to seam.

Fasten off.

Side seaming

NOTE: You can change the sleeve depth by working the side seaming and sleeve instructions for the size that suits you best.

Measure approx. 15 (17, 18.5, 20) (21.5, 21.5, 23) (25, 26, 28)cm/6 (6¾, 7¼, 8) (8½, 8½, 9) (9¾, 10¼, 11)in down from shoulder seam and place marker. With RS of both panels tog, join yarn in edge of Row 5 on either panel, ch1, 2sc through each row end on both panels to seam sides up to marker. At marker, turn RS out and work Sleeves.

Sleeves

Round 1: Ch3, evenly work 40 (44, 48, 52) (56, 56, 60) (64, 68, 72)dc around Sleeve edge, ss in ch-3 to join, turn. 40 (44, 48, 52) (56, 56, 60) (64, 68, 72) sts

Round 2: Ch3, dc2tog, 1dc in each rem st from prev row, ss to join, turn. 39 (43, 47, 51) (55, 55, 59) (63, 67, 71) sts

Rep Round 2 fifteen (seventeen, nineteen, nineteen) (twenty-three, twenty-three, twenty-seven) (twenty-seven, thirty-one, thirty-five) MORE times for a total of 17 (19, 21, 21) (25, 25, 29) (29, 33, 37) rows and 24 (26, 28, 32) (32, 32, 32) (36, 36, 36) sts.

NOTE: Stop the decreases sooner for a looser sleeve.

Round 3: Ch3, 1dc in each st, ss to join, turn.

Rep Round 3 approx. 20 (20, 18, 18) (14, 14, 10) (10, 6, 2) MORE times for a total of 38 (40, 40, 40) (40, 40, 40) (40, 40, 40) rows, or until your sleeve is 6cm (2¼in) longer than desired length.

Final round: Ch1, 1sc in each st.

Fasten off, fold cuff over and use yarn tail to secure it in place.

Bottom edging

With RS facing, join yarn in any st at back of work.

Round 1: Ch1, 1sc in each st around bottom edge of work to 1 st before side split, 3sc in final st, 2sc in each split row end, ss in seam, 2sc in each split row end, 3sc in first st at bottom of work, 1sc in each st along bottom edge. Rep as before for second split, then sc to ch-1, ss to join.

Fasten off and weave in all ends.

FLYING HIGH BATWING SWEATER

A beautiful, breezy sweater, perfect for those cooler summer days. Give a nod to the 80s with the classic batwing shape made in versatile neutrals. There are three different shades of green for the contrasting stripes, which are noted in the pattern just as CR rows – so you can choose in which order you would like to work the different colours.

Gauge (tension)

16 sts x 9 rows = 10 x 10cm (4 x 4in) using 4mm (US size G/6) hook.

Yarn & hook

Paintbox Yarns Simply DK (100% acrylic), DK (light worsted) weight yarn, 276m (302yd) per 100g (3½oz) ball in the following shades:

- Paper White (100) MC: 2 (2, 2¼, 3) (3¼, 3½, 3¾) (4¼, 4¼, 4¼) balls
- Spearmint Green (125); Pistachio Green (124); Washed Teal (132): 1 (1¼, 1¼, 1¾) (1¾, 1¾, 2) (2, 2, 2) balls of each CC

4mm (US size G/6) and 5.5mm (US size I/9) crochet hooks
2 stitch markers

	XXS	XS	S	M	L	XL	2X	3X	4X	5X
Waist circumference	62cm (24½in)	66.5cm (26¼in)	75.5cm (29¾in)	84.5cm (33¼in)	93cm (36½in)	115.5cm (45½in)	124cm (48¾in)	133cm (52¼in)	138cm (54¼in)	146.5cm (57¾in)
Length	45cm (17¾in)	50cm (19¾in)	50cm (19¾in)	55cm (21¾in)	55cm (21¾in)	55cm (21¾in)	55cm (21¾in)	60cm (23½in)	60cm (23½in)	60cm (23½in)
Cuff to cuff	102cm (40¼in)	122cm (48in)	122cm (48in)	140cm (55in)	140cm (55in)	144cm (56¾in)	157.5cm (62in)	160cm (63in)	160cm (63in)	160cm (63in)

Pattern notes & chart

As your body panels are worked in turned rows there is no right or wrong side, so just choose your favourite when seaming! The panels are worked in long rows from bottom hem, up and over the shoulder, and down to the hem again. You will work from the centre outward and crochet the sleeves directly onto the body panels without fastening off. Leave long yarn tails when working the sleeve rows to use when seaming.

Chart shows pattern repeat for guidance on stitch placement within the filet section only, place repeats within rows or rounds following written instructions for your chosen size. Read odd-number rows from right to left and even-number rows from left to right.

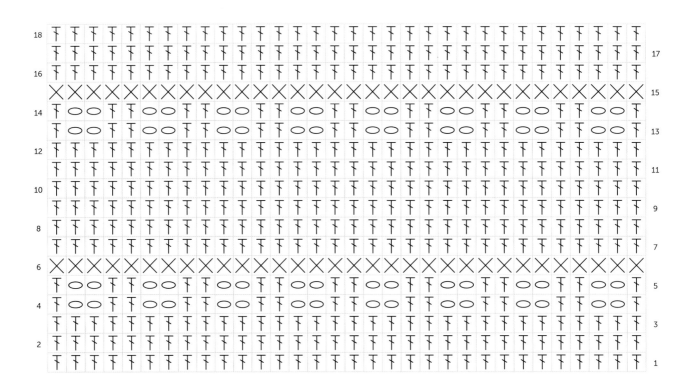

TIP: To alter the length change the length of your foundation row. It must be a multiple of four and be sure to start your sleeve shaping with the same number of sts open as stated in side seaming.

Body Panels
(make two)

Row 1: Using 4mm (US size G/6) hook and MC, fdc144 (160, 160, 176) (176, 176, 176) (192, 192, 192), turn.

OR: Using 4mm (US size G/6) hook and MC, ch147 (163, 163, 179) (179, 179, 179) (195, 195, 195), 1dc in fourth ch from hook and each ch along, turn.

Row 2: Ch3 (does not count as a st throughout), 1dc in each st, turn.

Row 3: Rep Row 2.

NOTE: Your work should be approx. double the finished length of your sweater, so don't panic at the length of it. Drape it over your shoulder to get an idea of how it will sit once done.

Row 4 (CR): Ch3, 1dc, *ch2, sk 2 sts, 2dc* to last 3 sts, ch2, sk 2 sts, 1dc, turn.

NOTE: For the CR (contrast rows) use CC 1 to 3 in your chosen order.

Row 5 (CR): Rep Row 4.

Row 6 (CR): Ch1, 1sc in each st, turn.

Rows 7–12: Rep Row 2.

Sizes XXS (XS) only:

Rep Row 4 two (three) more times for a total of 14 (15) rows.

Size (S) only:

Rep Rows 4–8 once more for a total of 17 rows.

Size (M) only :

Rep Rows 4–10 once more, for a total of 19 rows.

Size (L) only:

Rep Rows 4–12 once more, for a total of 21 rows.

Size (XL) only:

Rep Rows 4–12 once more, then rep Rows 4–8 once more for a total of 26 rows.

Size (2X) only:

Rep Rows 4–12 once more, then rep Rows 4–10 once more for a total of 28 rows.

Size (3X) only:

Rep Rows 4–12 twice more for a total of 30 rows.

Size (4X) only:

Rep Rows 4–12 twice more, then rep Row 4 once more for a total of 31 rows.

Size (5X) only:

Rep Rows 4–12 twice more, then rep Rows 4–6 once more for a total of 33 rows.

All sizes:

Side seaming

Fold piece in half at shoulder so stripes run top to bottom, 1sc through next 20 (22, 22, 25) (26, 26, 25) (34, 34, 33) sts on both edges to seam side leaving 104 (116, 116, 126) (124, 124, 126) (124, 124, 126) sts open for Sleeve. Turn RS out.

Sleeve shaping

Work foll dec rows as instructed for your size.

DC dec row (DCDR): Ch3, 1dc, dc2tog twice, 1dc to last 3 sts, dc2tog, 1dc, turn. (-3 sts)

SC dec row (SCDR): Ch1, 3sc, sc2tog, 1sc to last 5 sts, sc2tog, 3sc, turn. (-2 sts)

Size XXS only:

Row 1 (CR): SCDR.

Rows 2–7: DCDR.

Row 8 (CR): Ch3, 1dc, *ch2, sk 2 sts, 2dc* to last 3 sts, ch2, sk 2 sts, 1dc, turn.

Row 9 (CR): Rep Row 8.

Rep Rows 1–9 twice more, then rep Rows 1–5 once more for a total of 46 rows and 30 sts.

Move on to Cuff.

Size (XS) only:

Row 1 (CR): SCDR.

Rows 2–7: DCDR.

Row 8 (CR): Ch3, 1dc, *ch2, sk 2 sts, 2dc* to last 3 sts, ch2, sk 2 sts, 1dc, turn.

Row 9 (CR): Rep Row 8.

Rep Rows 1–9 three more times, then rep Rows 1 and 2 once more for a total of 53 rows and 31 sts.

Move on to Cuff.

Size (S) only:

Rows 1–4: DCDR.

Row 5 (CR): Ch3, 1dc, *ch2, sk 2 sts, 2dc* to last 3 sts, ch2, sk 2 sts, 1dc, turn.

Row 6 (CR): Rep Row 5.

Row 7 (CR): SCDR.

Rows 8–13: DCDR.

Rep Rows 5–13 twice more, then rep Rows 5–11 once more for a total of 55 rows and 30 sts.

Move on to Cuff.

Size (M) only:

Rows 1 and 2: DCDR.

Row 3 (CR): Ch3, 1dc, *ch2, sk 2 sts, 2dc* to last 3 sts, ch2, sk 2 sts, 1dc, turn.

Row 4 (CR): Rep Row 3.

Row 5 (CR): SCDR.

Rows 6–11: DCDR.

Rep Rows 3–11 three more times, then rep Rows 3–7 once more for a total of 62 rows and 32 sts.

Move on to Cuff.

Size (L) only:

Row 1 (CR): Ch3, 1dc, *ch2, sk 2 sts, 2dc* to last 3 sts, ch2, sk 2 sts, 1dc, turn.

Row 2 (CR): Rep Row 1.

Row 3 (CR): SCDR.

Rows 4–9: DCDR.

Rep Rows 1–9 three more times, then rep Rows 1–6 once more for a total of 63 rows and 33 sts.

Move on to Cuff.

Size (XL) only:

Rows 1–4: DCDR.

Row 5 (CR): Ch3, 1dc, *ch2, sk 2 sts, 2dc* to last 3 sts, ch2, sk 2 sts, 1dc, turn.

Row 6 (CR): Rep Row 5.

Row 7 (CR): SCDR.

Rows 8–13: DCDR.

Rep Rows 5–13 twice more, then rep Rows 5–12 once more for a total of 65 rows and 35 sts.

Move on to Cuff.

Size (2X) only:

Rows 1 and 2: DCDR.

Row 3 (CR): Ch3, 1dc, *ch2, sk 2 sts, 2dc* to last 3 sts, ch2, sk 2 sts, 1dc, turn.

Row 4 (CR): Rep Row 3.

Row 5 (CR): SCDR.

Rows 6–11: DCDR.

Rep Rows 3–11 three more times, then rep Rows 3–5 once more for a total of 69 rows and 38 sts.

Move on to Cuff.

Size (3X) only:

Row 1 (CR): Ch3, 1dc, *ch2, sk 2 sts, 2dc* to last 3 sts, ch2, sk 2 sts, 1dc, turn.

Row 2 (CR): Rep Row 1.

Row 3 (CR): SCDR.

Rows 4–9: DCDR.

Rep Rows 1–9 three more times, then rep Rows 1–5 once more for a total of 71 rows and 36 sts.

Move on to Cuff.

Size (4X) only:

Row 1 (CR): Ch3, 1dc, *ch2, sk 2 sts, 2dc* to last 3 sts, ch2, sk 2 sts, 1dc, turn.

Row 2 (CR): SCDR.

Rows 3–8: DCDR.

Row 9 (CR): Rep Row 1.

Rep Rows 1–9 three more times, then rep Rows 1–4 once more for a total of 71 rows and 36 sts.

Move on to Cuff.

Size (5X) only:

Rows 1–6: DCDR.

Row 7 (CR): Ch3, 1dc, *ch2, sk 2 sts, 2dc* to last 3 sts, ch2, sk 2 sts, 1dc, turn.

Row 8 (CR): Rep Row 7.

Row 9 (CR): SCDR.

Rep Rows 1–9 three more times, then rep Rows 1 and 2 once more for a total of 71 rows and 40 sts.

Move on to Cuff.

Cuff

Sizes XXS (S) (L, XL) (4X) only:

Row 1: Ch1, 1sc in each st.

Fasten off.

Sizes (XS) (2X) (5X) only:

Row 1: Ch3, 1dc in each st, turn.

Row 2: Rep Row 1.

Row 3: Ch1, 1sc in each st.

Fasten off.

Sizes (M) (3X) only:

Row 1: Ch3, 1dc in each st, turn.

Row 2: Ch3, sc in each st.

Fasten off.

Finishing

With RS tog, seam Sleeve edge using yarn tails starting at side seaming section and finishing at cuff.

With RS tog, lay both Body Panels flat next to each other with Sleeves at outside as if worn. Place marker where base of neckline should sit at both front and back of work. Join yarn at bottom hem and seam panels up to first marker by working 1sc through each st on both pieces to join.

Fasten off.

Repeat for second side, but at second marker turn RS out and work Neckline Edging.

Neckline edging

Round 1: Ch1, 1sc in each st around entire neckline, ss to join.

Fasten off.

Round 2: Using 5.5mm (US size I/9) hook and chosen CC, loosely ssBLO in each st, ss to join.

Fasten off.

Bottom edging

With RS facing, join yarn in row end by side seam.

Round 1: Ch1, 2sc in each row end around entire hem of work, ss in ch-1 to join, do not turn.

Round 2: Ch1, 1sc in each st, ss to join.

Fasten off and weave in all rem ends.

DILL PICKLES TEE

A super summer-friendly pattern, the Dill Pickles Tee will leave you pickled pink! Those staggered diamonds may look tricky, but trust me, this piece looks much more intricate than it really is. The simple repeats give an eye-catching and unique result, perfect for picnics in the park. Have a gherkin for me!

Gauge (tension)

16 sts x 9 rows = 10 x 10cm (4 x 4in) using 4mm (US size G/6) hook.

Yarn & hook

Paintbox Yarns Cotton DK (100% cotton), DK (light worsted) weight yarn, 125m (137yd) per 50g (1¾oz) ball in the following shade:
- Pistachio Green (425): 4¾ (5¾, 7¼, 8½) (9, 10, 10¾) (12¼, 13¼, 14) balls

4mm (US size G/6) crochet hook

2 stitch markers

	XXS	XS	S	M	L	XL	2X	3X	4X	5X
Circumference	75cm (29½in)	85cm (33½in)	95cm (37½in)	110cm (43½in)	117.5cm (46¼in)	127.5cm (50¼in)	140cm (55in)	147cm (58in)	160cm (63in)	170cm (67in)
Length	51cm (20in)	53cm (21in)	60cm (23½in)	62cm (24½in)	62cm (24½in)	62cm (24½in)	62cm (24½in)	66cm (26in)	66cm (26in)	66cm (26in)

Pattern notes & chart

As your body panels are worked in turned rows there is no right or wrong side, so just choose your favourite when seaming! For a shorter length, work less Diamond Section One repeats. For a longer length, work more Diamond Section One repeats. The turning ch1 does not count as a stitch throughout, but working a ch1 instead of ch3 will give your tee lovely smooth edges.

Chart shows pattern repeat for guidance on stitch placement within the filet section only, place repeats within rows or rounds following written instructions for your chosen size. Read odd-number rows from right to left and even-number rows from left to right.

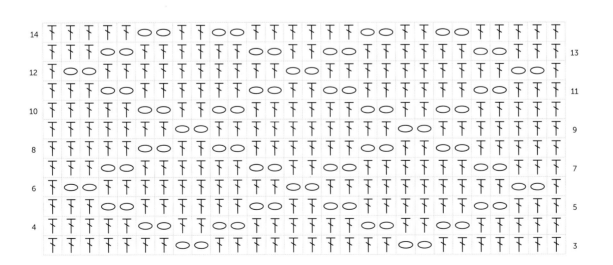

Back Panel

Row 1: Fdc60 (68, 76, 88) (94, 102, 112) (118, 128, 136), turn.

OR: Ch62 (70, 78, 90) (96, 104, 114) (120, 130, 138), 1dc in second ch from hook and each ch along, turn.

Row 2: Ch1 (does not count as a st throughout), 1dc in each st, turn.

Rep Row 2 zero (one, one, one) (one, one, one) (one, one, one) MORE times for a total of 2 (3, 3, 3) (3, 3, 3) (3, 3, 3) rows.

Sizes (XS, M) (L, 2X) (3X, 5X) only:

Diamond section one

Row 3: Ch1, (9, 7) (10, 7) (10, 7) dc, *ch2, sk 2 sts, 10dc* (4, 6) (6, 8) (8, 10) times, ch2, sk 2 sts, (9, 7) (10, 7) (10, 7)dc, turn.

Row 4: Ch1, (7, 5) (8, 5) (8, 5)dc, *ch2, sk 2 sts, 2dc, ch2, sk 2 sts, 6dc* (4, 6) (6, 8) (8, 10) times, ch2, sk 2 sts, 2dc, ch2, sk 2 sts, (7, 5) (8, 5) (8, 5)dc, turn.

Row 5: Ch1, (5, 3) (6, 3) (6, 3)dc, *ch2, sk 2 sts, 6dc, ch2, sk 2 sts, 2dc* (4, 6) (6, 8) (8, 10) times, ch2, sk 2 sts, 6dc, ch2, sk 2 sts, (5, 3) (6, 3) (6, 3)dc, turn.

Row 6: Ch1, (3, 1) (4, 1) (4, 1) dc, *ch2, sk 2 sts, 10dc* (5, 7) (7, 9) (9, 11) times, ch2, sk 2 sts, (3, 1) (4, 1) (4, 1)dc, turn.

Row 7: Rep Row 5.

Row 8: Rep Row 4.

Rep Diamond Section One (3, 2) (2, 1) (1, 0) MORE times then work Diamond Section Two.

Diamond section two

Row 9: Rep Row 3.

Row 10: Ch1, (11, 9) (12, 9) (12, 9) dc, *ch2, sk 2 sts, 6dc, ch2, sk 2 sts, 2dc* (3, 5) (5, 7) (7, 9) times, ch2, sk 2 sts, 6dc, ch2, sk 2 sts, (11, 9) (12, 9) (12, 9)dc, turn.

Row 11: Ch1, (13, 11) (14, 11) (14, 11)dc, *ch2, sk 2 sts, 2dc, ch2, sk 2 sts, 6dc* (3, 5) (5, 7) (7, 9) times, ch2, sk 2 sts, 2dc, ch2, sk 2 sts, (13, 11) (14, 11) (14, 11)dc, turn.

Row 12: Ch1, (15, 13) (16, 13) (16, 13)dc, *ch2, sk 2 sts, 10dc* (3, 5) (5, 7) (7, 9) times, ch2, sk 2 sts, (15, 13) (16, 13) (16, 13)dc, turn.

Row 13: Ch1, (17, 15) (18, 15) (18, 15)dc, *ch2, sk 2 sts, 6dc, ch2, sk 2 sts, 2dc* (2, 4) (4, 6) (6, 8) times, ch2, sk 2 sts, 6dc, ch2, sk 2 sts, (17, 15) (18, 15) (18, 15)dc, turn.

Row 14: Ch1, (19, 17) (20, 17) (20, 17)dc, *ch2, sk 2 sts, 2dc, ch2, sk 2 sts, 6dc* (2, 4) (4, 6) (6, 8) times, ch2, sk 2 sts, 2dc, ch2, sk 2 sts, (19, 17) (20, 17) (20, 17)dc, turn.

Row 15: Ch1, (21, 19) (22, 19) (22, 19)dc, *ch2, sk 2 sts, 10dc* (2, 4) (4, 6) (6, 8) times, ch2, sk 2 sts, (21, 19) (22, 19) (22, 19)dc, turn.

Row 16: Ch1, (23, 21) (24, 21) (24, 21)dc, *ch2, sk 2 sts, 6dc, ch2, sk 2 sts, 2dc* (1, 3) (3, 5) (5, 7) times, ch2, sk 2 sts, 6dc, ch2, sk 2 sts, (23, 21) (24, 21) (24, 21)dc, turn.

Row 17: Ch1, (25, 23) (26, 23) (26, 23)dc, *ch2, sk 2 sts, 2dc, ch2, sk 2 sts, 6dc* (1, 3) (3, 5) (5, 7) times, ch2, sk 2 sts, 2dc, ch2, sk 2 sts, (25, 23) (26, 23) (26, 23)dc, turn.

Row 18: Ch1, (27, 25) (28, 25) (28, 25)dc, *ch2, sk 2 sts, 10dc* (1, 3) (3, 5) (5, 7) times, ch2, sk 2 sts, (27, 25) (28, 25) (28, 25)dc, turn.

Size XS only:

Move on to Diamond Peak.

Sizes (M) (L, 2X) (3X, 5X) only:

Row 19: Ch1, (27) (30, 27) (30, 27)dc, *ch2, sk 2 sts, 6dc, ch2, sk 2 sts, 2dc* (2) (2, 4) (4, 6) times, ch2, sk 2 sts, 6dc, ch2, sk 2 sts, (27) (30, 27) (30, 27)dc, turn.

Row 20: Ch1, (29) (32, 29) (32, 29)dc, *ch2, sk 2 sts, 2dc, ch2, sk 2 sts, 6dc* (2) (2, 4) (4, 6) times, ch2, sk 2 sts, 2dc, ch2, sk 2 sts, (29) (32, 29) (32, 29)dc, turn.

Row 21: Ch1, (31) (34, 31) (34, 31)dc, *ch2, sk 2 sts, 10dc* (2) (2, 4) (4, 6) times, ch2, sk 2 sts, (31) (34, 31) (34, 31)dc, turn.

Row 22: Ch1, (33) (36, 33) (36, 33)dc, *ch2, sk 2 sts, 6dc, ch2, sk 2 sts, 2dc* (1) (1, 3) (3, 5) times, ch2, sk 2 sts, 6dc, ch2, sk 2 sts, (33) (36, 33) (36, 33)dc, turn.

Row 23: Ch1, (35) (38, 35) (38, 35)dc, *ch2, sk 2 sts, 2dc, ch2, sk 2 sts, 6dc* (1) (1, 3) (3, 5) times, ch2, sk 2 sts, 2dc, ch2, sk 2 sts, (35) (38, 35) (38, 35)dc, turn.

Row 24: Ch1, (37) (40, 37) (40, 37)dc, *ch2, sk 2 sts, 10dc* (1) (1, 3) (3, 5) times, ch2, sk 2 sts, (37) (40, 37) (40, 37)dc, turn.

Sizes (M) (L) only:

Move on to Diamond Peak.

Sizes (2X) (3X, 5X) only:

Row 25: Ch1, (39) (42, 39)dc, *ch2, sk 2 sts, 6dc, ch2, sk 2 sts, 2dc* (2) (2, 4) times, ch2, sk 2 sts, 6dc, ch2, sk 2 sts, (39) (42, 39)dc, turn.

Row 26: Ch1, (41) (44, 41)dc, *ch2, sk 2 sts, 2dc, ch2, sk 2 sts, 6dc* (2) (2, 4) times, ch2, sk 2 sts, 2dc, ch2, sk 2 sts, (41) (44, 41)dc, turn.

Row 27: Ch1, (43) (46, 43)dc, *ch2, sk 2 sts, 10dc* (2) (2, 4) times, ch2, sk 2 sts, (43) (46, 43)dc, turn.

Row 28: Ch1, (45) (48, 45)dc, *ch2, sk 2 sts, 6dc, ch2, sk 2 sts, 2dc* (1) (1, 3) times, ch2, sk 2 sts, 6dc, ch2, sk 2 sts, (45) (48, 45)dc, turn.

Row 29: Ch1, (47) (50, 47)dc, *ch2, sk 2 sts, 2dc, ch2, sk 2 sts, 6dc* (1) (1, 3) times, ch2, sk 2 sts, 2dc, ch2, sk 2 sts, (47) (50, 47)dc, turn.

Row 30: Ch1, (49) (52, 49)dc, *ch2, sk 2 sts, 10dc* (1) (1, 3) times, ch2, sk 2 sts, (49) (52, 49)dc, turn.

Sizes (2X) (3X) only:

Move on to Diamond Peak.

Size 5X only:

Row 31: Ch1, 51dc, *ch2, sk2 sts, 6dc, ch2, sk 2 sts, 2dc* twice, ch2, sk2 sts, 6dc, ch2, sk 2 sts, 51dc, turn.

Row 32: Ch1, 53dc, *ch2, sk 2 sts, 2dc, ch2, sk 2 sts, 6dc* twice, ch2, sk 2 sts, 2dc, ch2, sk 2 sts, 53dc, turn.

Row 33: Ch1, 55dc, *ch2, sk 2 sts, 10dc* twice, ch2, sk 2 sts, 55dc, turn.

Row 34: Ch1, 57dc, ch2, sk 2 sts, 6dc, ch2, sk 2 sts, 2dc, ch2, sk 2 sts, 6dc, ch2, sk 2 sts, 57dc, turn.

Row 35: Ch1, 59dc, ch2, sk 2 sts, 2dc, ch2, sk 2 sts, 6dc, ch2, sk 2 sts, 2dc, ch2, sk 2 sts, 59dc, turn.

Row 36: Ch1, 61dc, ch2, sk 2 sts, 10dc, ch2, sk 2 sts, 61dc, turn.

Move on to Diamond Peak.

Sizes XXS (S) (XL) (4X) only:

Diamond section one

Row 3: Ch1, 5 (1) (2) (3)dc, *ch2, sk 2 sts, 10dc* 4 (6) (8) (10) times, ch2, sk 2 sts, 5 (1) (2) (3)dc, turn.

Row 4: Ch1, 7 (3) (4) (5)dc, *ch2, sk 2 sts, 6dc, ch2, sk 2 sts, 2dc* 3 (5) (7) (9) times, ch2, sk 2 sts, 6dc, ch2, sk 2 sts, 7 (3) (4) (5)dc, turn.

Row 5: Ch1, 9 (5) (6) (7)dc, *ch2, sk 2 sts, 2dc, ch2, sk 2 sts, 6dc* 3 (5) (7) (9) times, ch2, sk 2 sts, 2dc, ch2, sk 2 sts, 9 (5) (6) (7)dc, turn.

Row 6: Ch1, 11 (7) (8) (9)dc, *ch2, sk 2 sts, 10dc* 3 (5) (7) (9) times, ch2, sk 2 sts, 11 (7) (8) (9)dc, turn.

Row 7: Rep Row 5.

Row 8: Rep Row 4.

Rep Diamond Section One 2 (2) (1) (0) MORE times then work Diamond Section Two.

Diamond section two

Rows 9–12: Rep Rows 3–6.

Row 13: Ch1, 13 (9) (10) (11)dc, *ch2, sk 2 sts, 6dc, ch2, sk 2 sts, 2dc* 2 (4) (6) (8) times, ch2, sk 2 sts, 6dc, ch2, sk 2 sts, 13 (9) (10) (11)dc, turn.

Row 14: Ch1, 15 (11) (12) (13)dc, *ch2, sk 2 sts, 2dc, ch2, sk 2 sts, 6dc* 2 (4) (6) (8) times, ch2, sk 2 sts, 2dc, ch2, sk 2 sts, 15 (11) (12) (13)dc, turn.

Row 15: Ch1, 17 (13) (14) (15) dc, *ch2, sk 2 sts, 10dc* 2 (4) (6) (8) times, ch2, sk 2 sts, 17 (13) (14) (15)dc, turn.

Row 16: Ch1, 19 (15) (16) (17)dc, *ch2, sk 2 sts, 6dc, ch2, sk 2 sts, 2dc* 1 (3) (5) (7) times, ch2, sk 2 sts, 6dc, ch2, sk 2 sts, 19 (15) (16) (17)dc, turn.

Row 17: Ch1, 21 (17) (18) (19)dc, *ch2, sk 2 sts, 2dc, ch2, sk 2 sts, 6dc* 1 (3) (5) (7) times, ch2, sk 2 sts, 2dc, ch2, sk 2 sts, 21 (17) (18) (19)dc, turn.

Row 18: Ch1, 23 (19) (20) (21)dc, *ch2, sk 2 sts, 10dc* 1 (3) (5) (7) times, ch2, sk 2 sts, 23 (19) (20) (21)dc, turn.

Size XXS only:

Move on to Diamond Peak.

Sizes (S) (XL) (4X) only:

Row 19: Ch1, (21) (22) (23)dc, *ch2, sk 2 sts, 6dc, ch2, sk 2 sts, 2dc* (2) (4) (6) times, ch2, sk 2 sts, 6dc, ch2, sk 2 sts, (21) (22) (23)dc, turn.

Row 20: Ch1, (23) (24) (25)dc, *ch2, sk 2 sts, 2dc, ch2, sk 2 sts, 6dc* (2) (4) (6) times, ch2, sk 2 sts, 2dc, ch2, sk 2 sts, (23) (24) (25)dc, turn.

Row 21: Ch1, (25) (26) (27)dc, *ch2, sk 2 sts, 10dc* (2) (4) (6) times, ch2, sk 2 sts, (25) (26) (27)dc, turn.

Row 22: Ch1, (27) (28) (29)dc, *ch2, sk 2 sts, 6dc, ch2, sk 2 sts, 2dc* (1) (3) (5) times, ch2, sk 2 sts, 6dc, ch2, sk 2 sts, (27) (28) (29)dc, turn.

Row 23: Ch1, (29) (30) (31)dc, *ch2, sk 2 sts, 2dc, ch2, sk 2 sts, 6dc* (1) (3) (5) times, ch2, sk 2 sts, 2dc, ch2, sk 2 sts, (29) (30) (31)dc, turn.

Row 24: Ch1, (31) (32) (33)dc, *ch2, sk 2 sts, 10dc* (1) (3) (5) times, ch2, sk 2 sts, (31) (32) (33)dc, turn.

Size (S) only:

Move on to Diamond Peak.

Sizes (XL) (4X) only:

Row 25: Ch1, (34) (35)dc, *ch2, sk 2 sts, 6dc, ch2, sk 2 sts, 2dc* (2) (4) times, ch2, sk 2 sts, 6dc, ch2, sk 2 sts, (34) (35)dc, turn.

Row 26: Ch1, (36) (37)dc, *ch2, sk 2 sts, 2dc, ch2, sk 2 sts, 6dc* (2) (4) times, ch2, sk 2 sts, 2dc, ch2, sk 2 sts, (36) (37)dc, turn.

Row 27: Ch1, (38) (39)dc, *ch2, sk 2 sts, 10dc* (2) (4) times, ch2, sk 2 sts, (38) (39)dc, turn.

Row 28: Ch1, (40) (41)dc, *ch2, sk 2 sts, 6dc, ch2, sk 2 sts, 2dc* (1) (3) times, ch2, sk 2 sts, 6dc, ch2, sk 2 sts, (40) (41)dc, turn.

Row 29: Ch1, (42) (43)dc, *ch2, sk 2 sts, 2dc, ch2, sk 2 sts, 6dc* (1) (3) times, ch2, sk 2 sts, 2dc, ch2, sk 2 sts, (42) (43)dc, turn.

Row 30: Ch1, (44) (45)dc, *ch2, sk 2 sts, 10dc* (1) (3) times, ch2, sk 2 sts, (44) (45)dc, turn.

Size (XL) only:

Move on to Diamond Peak.

Size 4X only:

Row 31: Ch1, 47dc, *ch2, sk 2 sts, 6dc, ch2, sk 2 sts, 2dc* twice, ch2, sk 2 sts, 6dc, ch2, sk 2 sts, 47dc, turn.

Row 32: Ch1, 49dc, *ch2, sk 2 sts, 2dc, ch2, sk 2 sts, 6dc* twice, ch2, sk 2 sts, 2dc, ch2, sk 2 sts, 49dc, turn.

Row 33: Ch1, 51dc, *ch2, sk 2 sts, 10dc* twice, ch2, sk 2 sts, 51dc, turn.

Row 34: Ch1, 53dc, ch2, sk 2 sts, 6dc, ch2, sk 2 sts, 2dc, ch2, sk 2 sts, 6dc, ch2, sk 2 sts, 53dc, turn.

Row 35: Ch1, 55dc, ch2, sk 2 sts, 2dc, ch2, sk 2 sts, 6dc, ch2, sk 2 sts, 2dc, ch2, sk 2 sts, 55dc, turn.

Row 36: Ch1, 57dc, ch2, sk 2 sts, 10dc, ch2, sk 2 sts, 57dc, turn.

All sizes:

Diamond peak

Row 1: Ch1, 25 (29, 33, 39) (42, 46, 51) (54, 59, 63)dc, ch2, sk 2 sts, 6dc, ch2, sk 2 sts, 25 (29, 33, 39) (42, 46, 51) (54, 59, 63)dc, turn.

Row 2: Ch1, 27 (31, 35, 41) (44, 48, 53) (56, 61, 65)dc, ch2, sk 2 sts,

2dc, ch2, sk 2 sts, 27 (31, 35, 41) (44, 48, 53) (56, 61, 65)dc, turn.

Row 3: Ch1, 29 (33, 37, 43) (46, 50, 55) (58, 63, 67)dc, ch2, sk 2 sts, 29 (33, 37, 43) (46, 50, 55) (58, 63, 67)dc, turn.

Upper body

Row 1: Ch1, 1dc in each st, turn.

Rep Row 1 twelve (thirteen, thirteen, fifteen) (fifteen, fifteen, fifteen) (nineteen, nineteen, nineteen) MORE times for a total of 13 (14, 14, 16) (16, 16, 16) (20, 20, 20) rows here and 46 (54, 54, 56) (56, 56, 56) (60, 60, 60) rows overall.

Fasten off.

Front Panel

Work as per Back Panel until end of Row 17 (17, 23, 23) (23, 29, 29) (29, 35, 35) then work Neckline One.

Neckline one

Row 1: Ch1, 23 (27, 31, 37) (40, 44, 49) (52, 57, 61)dc, ch2, sk 2 sts, 4dc, turn. 29 (33, 37, 43) (46, 50, 55) (58, 63, 67) sts

Row 2: Ch1, 1dc, dc2tog, 1dc in each rem st, turn. 28 (32, 36, 42) (45, 49, 54) (57, 62, 66) sts

Row 3: Ch1, 1dc to last 3 sts, dc2tog, 1dc, turn. 27 (31, 35, 41) (44, 48, 53) (56, 61, 65) sts

Rep Rows 2 and 3 six (five, six, six) (six, seven, seven) (eight, eight, eight) MORE times.

Sizes (XS, S, M) (L) (4X, 5X) only:

Rep Row 2 once more for a total of (14, 14, 16) (16) (20, 20) rows for Neckline One and (20, 22, 28) (31) (44, 48) sts.

Sizes XXS (XL, 2X) only:

A total of 15 (17, 17) rows for Neckline One and 15 (34, 39) sts.

Move to Row 5.

All other sizes:

Row 4: Ch1, 1dc in each st, turn.

Size 3X only:

Rep Row 4 once more for a total of 21 rows for Neckline One and 40 sts.

All sizes:

Row 5: Ch1, with RS of Front and Back Panels tog, 1sc through next 15 (20, 22, 28) (31, 34, 39) (30, 43, 48) sts on both edges to seam shoulder.

Fasten off and work Neckline Two.

Neckline two

With RS facing, count 2 sts from end of Neckline One Row 1 and join yarn in next st.

Row 1: Ch1, 4dc, ch2, sk 2 sts, 1dc in each rem st, turn.

Row 2: Ch1, 1dc to last 3 sts, dc2tog, 1dc, turn. 28 (32, 36, 42) (45, 49, 54) (57, 62, 66) sts

Row 3: Ch1, 1dc, dc2tog, 1dc in each rem st, turn. 27 (31, 35, 41) (44, 48, 53) (56, 61, 65) sts

Rep Rows 2 and 3 six (five, six, six) (six, seven, seven) (eight, eight, eight) MORE times.

Sizes (XS, S, M) (L) (4X, 5X) only:

Rep Row 2 once more for a total of (14, 14, 16) (16) (20, 20) rows for Neckline Two and (20, 22, 28) (31) (44, 48) sts.

Sizes XXS (XL) (2X) only:

A total of 15 (17, 17) rows for Neckline Two and 15 (34, 39) sts.

Move to Row 5.

All other sizes:

Row 4: Ch1, 1dc in each st, turn.

Size 3X only:

Rep Row 4 once more for a total of 21 rows for Neckline Two and 40 sts.

All sizes:

Row 5: Ch1, with RS of Front and Back Panels tog, 1sc through next 15 (20, 24, 28) (31, 34, 39) (40, 43, 48) sts on both edges to seam shoulder.

Fasten off.

Finishing

With RS tog, lay piece flat and measure desired armhole depth (approx. 16 (18, 19, 20) (21, 22, 24) (24, 25, 26)cm/6¼ (7, 7½, 8) (8¼, 8¾, 9½) (9½, 9¾, 10¼)in) down from shoulder seam. Place marker through both panels, making sure to mark same row on both sides.

Join yarn in Row 3 (4, 4, 4) (4, 4, 4) (4, 4, 4) at start of Diamond Section One, work approx. 2sc through each row end on both panels to seam side to marker. At marker, turn RS out.

Round 1: Ch1, work 2sc in each row edge around armhole, ss in ch-1 to join.

Fasten off.

Repeat for second side.

Neckline edging

With RS facing, join yarn in any st at back of neckline.

Round 1: Ch1, 1sc loosely in each st at back of neckline, 2sc in each Neckline One row end, 1sc in 2 sts at front of neckline, 2sc in each Neckline Two row end, 1sc in each rem st at back of neckline, ss in ch-1 to join.

Fasten off and weave in all ends.

FESTIVE FIRS SWEATER

The perfect make to keep you cosy through the holidays, Festive Firs is a subtle but fun take on the classic Christmas sweater. It's the perfect mix of kitsch and cute for a sweater you'll bring out year after year. If you don't want a festive sweater, the firs motifs are interchangeable with the hearts from the Time After Time Sweater – see Pattern Notes for more information.

Gauge (tension)

13 sts x 7 rows = 10 x 10cm (4 x 4in) using 5mm (US size H/8) hook.

Yarn & hook

Paintbox Yarns Simply Aran (100% acrylic), aran (worsted) weight yarn, 184m (201yd) per 100g (3½oz) ball in the following shades:

- Slate Green (226) MC: 5 (5¾, 6¼, 6½) (7, 7½, 9) (9½, 10¼, 10¾) balls
- Buttercup Yellow (222) CC: ¼ (¼, ¼, ¼) (¼, ¼, ½) (½, ½, ½) ball

5mm (US size H/8) crochet hook

	XXS	XS	S	M	L	XL	2X	3X	4X	5X
Circumference	92.5cm (36½in)	101.5cm (40in)	108cm (42½in)	117cm (46in)	132.5cm (52¼in)	141.5cm (55¾in)	151cm (59¼in)	163cm (64¼in)	175.5cm (69in)	188cm (74in)
Length	47cm (18½in)	57cm (22½in)	57cm (22½in)	57cm (22½in)	57cm (22½in)	57cm (22½in)	67cm (26½in)	67cm (26½in)	67cm (26½in)	67cm (26½in)
Sleeve depth	19.5cm (7¾in)	19.5cm (7¾in)	22cm (8¾in)	22cm (8¾in)	22cm (8¾in)	22cm (8¾in)	26cm (10¼in)	26cm (10¼in)	27cm (10½in)	27cm (10½in)

Pattern notes & chart

This pattern is written a little differently to most others because the tree motifs can be swapped for the hearts by working the heart pattern repeat between the two * from the Time After Time Sweater.

Chart shows pattern repeat for guidance on stitch placement within the filet section only, place repeats within rows or rounds following written instructions for your chosen size. Read RS (even-number) rows from left to right and WS (odd-number) rows from right to left.

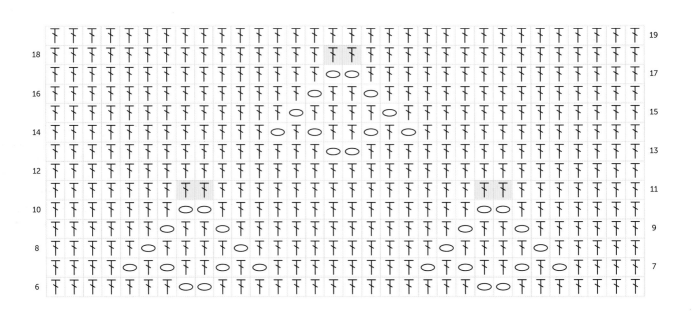

TIP: To make this sweater in DK (light worsted) yarn, follow the instructions from the Time After Time sweater, but use the pattern repeat between the two * from this sweater. Be sure to work the repeat in full, because there are stitches before and after the filet in each row.

Back Panel

Row 1: Using MC, fdc60 (66, 70, 76) (86, 92, 98) (106, 114, 122), turn.

OR: Using MC, ch63 (69, 73, 79) (89, 95, 101) (109, 117, 125), 1dc in fourth ch from hook and each ch along, turn.

Row 2: Ch3 (does not count as a st throughout), 1dc in each st, turn.

Row 3: Rep Row 2.

Rows 4 and 5: Rep Row 2.

Tree section one

Row 6 (RS): Ch3, 6 (1, 3, 6) (3, 6, 1) (5, 1, 5)dc, *7dc, ch2, sk 2 sts, 7dc* 3 (4, 4, 4) (5, 5, 6) (6, 7, 7) times, 6 (1, 3, 6) (3, 6, 1) (5, 1, 5)dc, turn.

Row 7 (WS): Ch3, 6 (1, 3, 6) (3, 6, 1) (5, 1, 5)dc, *4dc, ch1, sk 1 st, 1dc, ch1, sk 1 st, 2dc, ch1, sk 1 st, 1dc, ch1, sk 1 st, 4dc* 3 (4, 4, 4) (5, 5, 6) (6, 7, 7) times, 6 (1, 3, 6) (3, 6, 1) (5, 1, 5)dc, turn.

Row 8: Ch3, 6 (1, 3, 6) (3, 6, 1) (5, 1, 5)dc, *5dc, ch1, sk 1 st, 4dc, ch1, sk 1 st, 5dc* 3 (4, 4, 4) (5, 5, 6) (6, 7, 7) times, 6 (1, 3, 6) (3, 6, 1) (5, 1, 5)dc, turn.

Row 9: Ch3, 6 (1, 3, 6) (3, 6, 1) (5, 1, 5)dc, *6dc, ch1, sk 1 st, 2dc, ch1, sk 1 st, 6dc* 3 (4, 4, 4) (5, 5, 6) (6, 7, 7) times, 6 (1, 3, 6) (3, 6, 1) (5, 1, 5)dc, turn.

Row 10: Ch3, 6 (1, 3, 6) (3, 6, 1) (5, 1, 5)dc, *7dc, ch2, sk 2 sts, 7dc* 3 (4, 4, 4) (5, 5, 6) (6, 7, 7) times, 6 (1, 3, 6) (3, 6, 1) (5, 1, 5)dc, turn.

Row 11: Ch3, 6 (1, 3, 6) (3, 6, 1) (5, 1, 5)dc, *7dc in MC, 2dc in CC, 7dc in MC* 3 (4, 4, 4) (5, 5, 6) (6, 7, 7) times, 6 (1, 3, 6) (3, 6, 1) (5, 1, 5)dc, turn.

Row 12: Ch3, 1dc in each st, turn.

NOTE: When using the CC, fasten off each time, knot the ends on the WS and weave in. The CC is used on both RS and WS rows, so tails may be at the back or the front.

Tree section two

Row 13: Ch3, 14 (9, 11, 14) (11, 14, 9) (13, 9, 13)dc, *7dc, ch2, sk 2 sts, 7dc* 2 (3, 3, 3) (4, 4, 5) (5, 6, 6) times, 14 (9, 11, 14) (11, 14, 9) (13, 9, 13)dc, turn.

Row 14: Ch3, 14 (9, 11, 14) (11, 14, 9) (13, 9, 13)dc, *4dc, ch1, sk 1 st, 1dc, ch1, sk 1 st, 2dc, ch1, sk 1 st, 1dc, ch1, sk 1 st, 4dc* 2 (3, 3, 3) (4, 4, 5) (5, 6, 6) times, 14 (9, 11, 14) (11, 14, 9) (13, 9, 13)dc, turn.

Row 15: Ch3, 14 (9, 11, 14) (11, 14, 9) (13, 9, 13)dc, *5dc, ch1, sk 1 st, 4dc, ch1, sk 1 st, 5dc* 2 (3, 3, 3) (4, 4, 5) (5, 6, 6) times, 14 (9, 11, 14) (11, 14, 9) (13, 9, 13)dc, turn.

Row 16: Ch3, 14 (9, 11, 14) (11, 14, 9) (13, 9, 13)dc, *6dc, ch1, sk 1 st, 2dc, ch1, sk 1 st, 6dc* 2 (3, 3, 3) (4, 4, 5) (5, 6, 6) times, 14 (9, 11, 14) (11, 14, 9) (13, 9, 13)dc, turn.

Row 17: Ch3, 14 (9, 11, 14) (11, 14, 9) (13, 9, 13)dc, *7dc, ch2, sk 2 sts, 7dc* 2 (3, 3, 3) (4, 4, 5) (5, 6, 6) times, 14 (9, 11, 14) (11, 14, 9) (13, 9, 13)dc, turn.

Row 18: Ch3, 14 (9, 11, 14) (11, 14, 9) (13, 9, 13)dc, *7dc in MC, 2dc in CC, 7dc in MC* 2 (3, 3, 3) (4, 4, 5) (5, 6, 6) times, 14 (9, 11, 14) (11, 14, 9) (13, 9, 13)dc, turn.

Row 19: Ch3, 1dc in each st, turn.

Rep Tree Sections One and Two 1 (1, 1, 1) (1, 1, 2) (2, 2, 2) MORE times.

Sizes (XS, S, M) (L, XL) only:

Rep Tree Section One once more.

All sizes:

There is now a total of 33 (40, 40, 40) (40, 40, 47) (47, 47, 47) rows.

Fasten off.

Front Panel

Work as per Back Panel until one Tree Section short of finished length, then work Neckline One.

Neckline one

Size XXS only:

Row 1: Ch3, 20dc, turn.

Row 2: Ch3, 1dc in each st, turn.

Rows 3–7: Rep Row 2.

Row 8: Ch1, with RS of both panels tog, 1sc through next 20 sts on both edges to seam shoulder.

Fasten off and work Neckline Two.

Sizes (XS, S, M) (L, XL) only:

Row 1: Ch3, (1, 3, 6) (3, 6)dc, *7dc, ch2, sk 2 sts, 7dc* once, (6, 6, 6) (14, 14)dc, turn.

Row 2: Ch3, (6, 6, 6) (14, 14)dc, *4dc, ch1, sk 1 st, 1dc, ch1, sk 1 st, 2dc, ch1, sk 1 st, 1dc, ch1, sk 1 st, 4dc* once, (1, 3, 6) (3, 6)dc, turn.

Row 3: Ch3, (1, 3, 6) (3, 6)dc, *5dc, ch1, sk 1 st, 4dc, ch1, sk 1 st, 5dc* once, (6, 6, 6) (14, 14)dc, turn.

Row 4: Ch3, (6, 6, 6) (14, 14)dc, *6dc, ch1, sk 1 st, 2dc, ch1, sk 1 st, 6dc* once, (1, 3, 6) (3, 6)dc, turn.

Row 5: Ch3, (1, 3, 6) (3, 6)dc, *7dc, ch2, sk 2 sts, 7dc* once, (6, 6, 6) (14, 14)dc, turn.

Row 6: Ch3, (6, 6, 6) (14, 14)dc, *7dc in MC, 2dc in CC, 7dc in MC* once, (1, 3, 6) (3, 6)dc, turn.

Row 7: Ch3, 1dc in each st, turn.

Row 8: Ch1, with RS of both panels tog, 1sc through next (23, 25, 28) (33, 36) sts on both edges to seam shoulder.

Fasten off and work Neckline Two.

Sizes (2X) (3X, 4X, 5X) only:

Row 1: Ch3, (9) (13, 9, 13)dc, *7dc, ch2, sk 2 sts, 7dc* (1) (1, 2, 2) times, (14) (13, 5, 5)dc, turn.

Row 2: Ch3, (14) (13, 5, 5)dc, *4dc, ch1, sk 1 st, 1dc, ch1, sk 1 st, 2dc, ch1, sk 1 st, 1dc, ch1, sk 1 st, 4dc* (1) (1, 2, 2) times, (9) (13, 9, 13)dc, turn.

Row 3: Ch3, (9) (13, 9, 13)dc, *5dc, ch1, sk 1 st, 4dc, ch1, sk 1 st, 5dc* (1) (1, 2, 2) times, (14) (13, 5, 5)dc, turn.

Row 4: Ch3, (14) (13, 5, 5)dc, *6dc, ch1, sk 1 st, 2dc, ch1, sk 1 st, 6dc* (1) (1, 2, 2) times, (9) (13, 9, 13)dc, turn.

Row 5: Ch3, (9) (13, 9, 13) dc, *7dc, ch2, sk 2 sts, 7dc* (1) (1, 2, 2) times, (14) (13, 5, 5)dc, turn.

Row 6: Ch3, (14) (13, 5, 5)dc, *7dc in MC, 2dc in CC, 7dc in MC* (1) (1, 2, 2) times, (9) (13, 9, 13)dc, turn.

Row 7: Ch3, 1dc in each st, turn.

Row 8: Ch1, with RS of both panels tog, 1sc through next (39) (42, 46, 50) sts on both edges to seam shoulder.

Fasten off.

Neckline two

Cont in st pattern, count 20 (23, 25, 28) (33, 36, 39) (42, 46, 50) sts from other edge of work and join yarn.

Size XXS only:

Row 1: Ch3, 20dc, turn.

Row 2: Ch3, 1dc in each st, turn.

Rows 3–7: Rep Row 2.

Row 8: Ch1, with RS of both panels tog, 1sc through next 20 sts on both edges to seam shoulder.

Fasten off.

Sizes (XS, S, M) (L, XL) only:

Row 1: Ch3, (6, 6, 6) (14, 14) dc, *7dc, ch2, sk 2 sts, 7dc* once, (1, 3, 6) (3, 6)dc, turn.

Row 2: Ch3, (1, 3, 6) (3, 6) dc, *4dc, ch1, sk 1 st, 1dc, ch1, sk 1 st, 2dc, ch1, sk 1 st, 1dc, ch1, sk 1 st, 4dc* once, (6, 6, 6) (14, 14)dc, turn.

Row 3: Ch3, (6, 6, 6) (14, 14)dc, *5dc, ch1, sk 1 st, 4dc, ch1, sk 1 st, 5dc* once, (1, 3, 6) (3, 6)dc, turn.

Row 4: Ch3, (1, 3, 6) (3, 6)dc, *6dc, ch1, sk 1 st, 2dc, ch1, sk 1 st, 6dc* once, (6, 6, 6) (14, 14)dc, turn.

Row 5: Ch3, (6, 6, 6) (14, 14) dc, *7dc, ch2, sk 2 sts, 7dc* once, (1, 3, 6) (3, 6)dc, turn.

Row 6: Ch3, (1, 3, 6) (3, 6)dc, *7dc in MC, 2dc in CC, 7dc in MC* once, (6, 6, 6) (14, 14)dc, turn.

Row 7: Ch3, 1dc in each st, turn.

Row 8: ch1, with RS of both panels tog, 1sc through next (23, 25, 28) (33, 36) sts on both edges to seam shoulder.

Fasten off.

Sizes (2X) (3X, 4X, 5X) only:

Row 1: Ch3, (14) (13, 5, 5)dc, *7dc, ch2, sk 2 sts, 7dc* (1) (1, 2, 2) times, (9) (13, 9, 13)dc, turn.

Row 2: Ch3, (9) (13, 9, 13)dc, *4dc, ch1, sk 1 st, 1dc, ch1, sk 1 st, 2dc, ch1, sk 1 st, 1dc, ch1, sk 1 st, 4dc* (1) (1, 2, 2) times, (14) (13, 5, 5)dc, turn.

Row 3: Ch3, (14) (13, 5, 5)dc, *5dc, ch1, sk 1 st, 4dc, ch1, sk 1 st, 5dc* (1) (1, 2, 2) times, (9) (13, 9, 13)dc, turn.

Row 4: Ch3, (9) (13, 9, 13)dc, *6dc, ch1, sk 1 st, 2dc, ch1, sk 1 st, 6dc* (1) (1, 2, 2) times, (14) (13, 5, 5)dc, turn.

Row 5: Ch3, (14) (13, 5, 5)dc, *7dc, ch2, sk 2 sts, 7dc* (1) (1, 2, 2) times, (9) (13, 9, 13)dc, turn.

Row 6: Ch3, (9) (13, 9, 13)dc, *7dc in MC, 2dc in CC, 7dc in MC* (1) (1, 2, 2) times, (14) (13, 5, 5)dc, turn.

Row 7: Ch3, 1dc in each st, turn.

Row 8: Ch1, with RS of Front and Back Panels tog, 1sc through next (39) (42, 46, 50) sts on both edges to seam shoulder.

Fasten off.

Sleeves
(make two)

Round 1: Using MC, ch25 (25, 28, 28) (28, 28, 30) (30, 32, 32), ss to join into a ring.

Round 2: Ch3 (does not count as a st throughout), 1dc in each st, ss to join, turn.

Round 3: Rep Round 2.

Sizes XXS (XS, S, M) (L, XL) only:

Round 4: Ch3, 2dc in each st, ss to join, turn. 50 (50, 56, 56) (56, 56) sts

Sizes (2X) (3X, 4X, 5X) only:

Round 4: Ch3, 2dc in first st, [2dc in each of next 4 sts, 3dc in next st] 5 times, 2dc in each of next (3) (3, 5, 5) sts, 3dc in next st, ss to join, turn. (66) (66, 70, 70) sts

All sizes:

Round 5: Ch3, 1dc in each st, ss to join, turn.

Tree section one

Round 6: Ch3, 1 (1, 4, 4) (4, 4, 1) (1, 3, 3)dc, *7dc, ch2, sk 2 sts, 7dc* 3 (3, 3, 3) (3, 3, 4) (4, 4, 4) times, 1 (1, 4, 4) (4, 4, 1) (1, 3, 3)dc, ss to join, turn.

Round 7: Ch3, 1 (1, 4, 4) (4, 4, 1) (1, 3, 3)dc, *4dc, ch1, sk 1 st, 1dc, ch1, sk 1 st, 2dc, ch1, sk 1 st, 1dc, ch1, sk 1 st, 4dc* 3 (3, 3, 3) (3, 3, 4) (4, 4, 4) times, 1 (1, 4, 4) (4, 4,

1) (1, 3, 3)dc, ss to join, turn.

Round 8: Ch3, 1 (1, 4, 4) (4, 4, 1) (1, 3, 3)dc, *5dc, ch1, sk 1 st, 4dc, ch1, sk 1 st, 5dc* 3 (3, 3, 3) (3, 3, 4) (4, 4, 4) times, 1 (1, 4, 4) (4, 4, 1) (1, 3, 3)dc, ss to join, turn.

Round 9: Ch3, 1 (1, 4, 4) (4, 4, 1) (1, 3, 3)dc, *6dc, ch1, sk 1 st, 2dc, ch1, sk 1 st, 6dc* 3 (3, 3, 3) (3, 3, 4) (4, 4, 4) times, 1 (1, 4, 4) (4, 4, 1) (1, 3, 3)dc, ss to join, turn.

Round 10: Ch3, 1 (1, 4, 4) (4, 4, 1) (1, 3, 3)dc, *7dc, ch2, sk 2 sts, 7dc* 3 (3, 3, 3) (3, 3, 4) (4, 4, 4) times, 1 (1, 4, 4) (4, 4, 1) (1, 3, 3)dc, ss to join, turn.

Round 11: Ch3, 1 (1, 4, 4) (4, 4, 1) (1, 3, 3)dc, *7dc in MC, 2dc in CC, 7dc in MC* 3 (3, 3, 3) (3, 3, 4) (4, 4, 4) times, 1 (1, 4, 4) (4, 4, 1) (1, 3, 3)dc, ss to join, turn.

Round 12: Ch3, 1dc in each st, ss to join, turn.

Tree section two

Round 13: Ch3, 9 (9, 12, 12) (12, 12, 9) (9, 11, 11)dc, *7dc, ch2, sk 2 sts, 7dc* 2 (2, 2, 2) (2, 2, 3) (3, 3, 3) times, 9 (9, 12, 12) (12, 12, 9) (9, 11, 11)dc, ss to join, turn.

Round 14: Ch3, 9 (9, 12, 12) (12, 12, 9) (9, 11, 11)dc, *4dc, ch1, sk 1 st, 1dc, ch1, sk 1 st, 2dc, ch1, sk 1 st, 1dc, ch1, sk 1 st, 4dc* 2 (2, 2, 2) (2, 2, 3) (3, 3, 3) times, 9 (9, 12, 12) (12, 12, 9) (9, 11, 11)dc, ss to join, turn.

Round 15: Ch3, 9 (9, 12, 12) (12, 12, 9) (9, 11, 11)dc, *5dc, ch1, sk 1 st, 4dc, ch1, sk 1 st, 5dc* 2 (2, 2, 2) (2, 2, 3) (3, 3, 3) times, 9 (9, 12, 12) (12, 12, 9) (9, 11, 11)dc, ss to join, turn.

Round 16: Ch3, 9 (9, 12, 12) (12, 12, 9) (9, 11, 11)dc, *6dc, ch1, sk 1 st, 2dc, ch1, sk 1 st, 6dc* 2 (2, 2, 2) (2, 2, 3) (3, 3, 3) times, 9 (9, 12, 12) (12, 12, 9) (9, 11, 11)dc, ss to join, turn.

Round 17: Ch3, 9 (9, 12, 12) (12, 12, 9) (9, 11, 11)dc, *7dc, ch2, sk 2 sts, 7dc* 2 (2, 2, 2) (2, 2, 3) (3, 3, 3) times, 9 (9,

TIP: You could repeat Row 19 at the end of your final Tree Section Two on the Sleeves for additional length without adding a whole extra repeat.

12, 12) (12, 12, 9) (9, 11, 11)dc, turn.

Round 18: Ch3, 9 (9, 12, 12) (12, 12, 9) (9, 11, 11)dc, *7dc in MC, 2dc in CC, 7dc in MC* 2 (2, 2, 2) (2, 2, 3) (3, 3, 3) times, 9 (9, 12, 12) (12, 12, 9) (9, 11, 11)dc, turn.

Round 19: Ch3, 1dc in each st, ss to join, turn.

Rep Tree Sections One and Two once more for a total of 33 rows, or until Sleeve is desired length, then fasten off.

Finishing

Seam sides and join Sleeves to body panels.

Neckline edging

With RS facing join yarn in any st at back of neckline.

Round 1: Ch3, 1dc in each st at back of neckline, 2dc in each neckline row end, 1dc in each st at front of neckline, 2dc in each neckline row end as before, 1dc in each rem st at back of neckline, ss to join, do not turn.

Round 2: Ch1, 1sc in each st, ss to join.

Fasten off and weave in ends.

BILLIE JEAN BOATNECK SWEATER

A super simple but interesting sweater that showcases the beauty of filet perfectly! Fun bobbles add texture to the basic shape, and the mesh-like filet makes for a perfect transitional piece. Ideal for those bright but chilly summer evenings in the garden with a glass of fizz.

Gauge (tension)

16 sts x 9 rows = 10 x 10cm (4 x 4in) using 4mm (US size G/6) hook.

Yarn & hook

Paintbox Yarns Simply DK (100% acrylic), DK (light worsted) weight yarn, 276m (302yd) per 100g (3½oz) ball in the following shade:
• Vanilla Cream (107): 2½ (2¾, 3¼, 3¾) (4, 4½, 5) (5¼, 6, 6¼) balls
4mm (US size G/6) and 6mm (US size J/10) crochet hooks

	XXS	XS	S	M	L	XL	2X	3X	4X	5X
Circumference	78cm (30¾in)	87.5cm (34½in)	96cm (37¾in)	105cm (41¼in)	114cm (45in)	122.5cm (48¼in)	131cm (51½in)	140cm (55in)	149cm (58¾in)	157.5cm (62in)
Length	45.5cm (18in)	45.5cm (18in)	52cm (20½in)	52cm (20½in)	52cm (20½in)	59cm (23¼in)	59cm (23¼in)	59cm (23¼in)	66.5cm (26¼in)	66.5cm (26¼in)
Sleeve depth	15cm (6in)	17.5cm (7in)	17.5cm (7in)	20cm (8in)	22cm (8¾in)	22cm (8¾in)	24cm (9½in)	26cm (10¼in)	26cm (10¼in)	28.5cm (11¼in)

Pattern notes & chart

Chart shows pattern repeat for guidance on stitch placement within the filet section only, place repeats within rows or rounds following written instructions for your chosen size. Read RS (even-number) rows from left to right and WS (odd-number) rows from right to left.

Special abbreviation

Bobble: [yo, insert hook into st, yo, pull through st, yo, pull through 2 loops on hook] 4 times, yo, pull through all remaining loops on hook

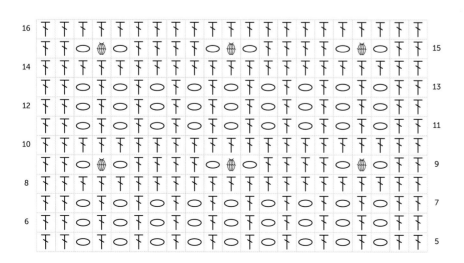

TIP: As usual, you can easily alter the length of this jumper by working more or fewer pattern repeats.

Back Panel

Row 1: Using 4mm (US size G/6) hook, fdc63 (70, 77, 84) (91, 98, 105) (112, 119, 126), turn.

OR: Using 4mm (US size G/6) hook, ch66 (73, 80, 87) (94, 101, 108) (115, 122, 129), 1dc in fourth ch from hook and each ch along, turn.

Row 2: Ch3 (does not count as a st throughout), 1dc in each st, turn.

Rows 3 and 4: Rep Row 2.

Row 5: Ch3, 2dc, *ch1, sk 1 st, 1dc* to last st, 1dc in final st, turn.

Rows 6 and 7: Rep Row 5.

Row 8: Ch3, 1dc in each st, turn.

Row 9 (WS): Ch3, 2dc *ch1, sk 1 st, bobble, ch1, sk 1 st, 4dc*, to last 5 sts, ch1, sk 1 st, bobble, ch1, sk 1 st, 2dc, turn.

Row 10: Rep Row 8.

Rep Rows 5–10 five (five, six, six) (six, seven, seven) (seven, eight, eight) MORE times, then rep Row 8 once more for a total of 41 (41, 47, 47) (47, 53, 53) (53, 59, 59) rows.

Fasten off, leaving a long tail for seaming.

Front Panel

Work as per Back Panel to two rows short of finished length, then work Neckline Shaping.

Neckline shaping

Row 1: Ch3, 14 (16, 19, 22) (25, 28, 31) (34, 37, 40)dc, 35 (38, 39, 40) (41, 42, 43) (44, 45, 46)sc, 14 (16, 19, 22) (25, 28, 31) (34, 37, 40)dc, turn.

Row 2: Rep Row 1.

Fasten off, leaving a long tail for seaming.

Sleeves
(make two)

Row 1: Using 4mm (US size G/6) hook, fdc49 (56, 56, 63) (63, 63, 63) (63, 63, 63), turn.

OR: Using 4mm (US size G/6) hook, ch52 (59, 59, 66) (66, 66, 66) (66, 66, 66), 1dc in fourth ch from hook and each ch along, turn.

Row 2: Ch3 (does not count as a st throughout), 1dc in each st, turn.

Rows 3 and 4: Rep Row 2.

Row 5: Ch3, 2dc, *ch1, sk 1 st, 1dc* to last st, 1dc, turn.

Rows 6 and 7: Rep Row 5.

Row 8: Ch3, 1dc in each st, turn.

Row 9 (WS): Ch3, 2dc *ch1, sk 1 st, bobble, ch1, sk 1 st, 4dc*, to last 5 sts, ch1, sk 1 st, bobble, ch1, sk 1 st, 2dc, turn.

Row 10: Rep Row 8.

Sizes XXS (XS, S, M) only:

Rep Rows 5–10 two MORE times.

Fasten off, leaving a long tail.

Sizes (L, XL) only:

Rows 11–16: Rep Rows 5–10.

Row 17: Rep Row 5.

Row 18: Rep Row 6.

Row 19: Ch3, 2dc in first st, 1dc, *ch1, sk 1 st, 1dc* to last st, 2dc in final st, turn. (65, 65) sts

Row 20: Ch3, 2dc in the first st, 1dc in each st to last st, 2dc in final st, turn. (67, 67) sts

Row 21: Ch3, 2dc in first st, 3dc *ch1, sk 1 st, bobble, ch1, sk 1 st, 4dc*, to last 7 sts, ch1, sk 1 st, bobble, ch1, sk 1 st, 3dc, 2dc in final st, turn. (69, 69) sts

Row 22: Ch3, 2dc in first st, 1dc in each st to end. (70, 70) sts

Fasten off, leaving a long tail.

Size (2X) only

Rows 11–15: Rep Rows 5–9.

Row 16: Ch3, 2dc in first st, 1dc in each st to last st, 2dc in final st, turn. (65) sts

Row 17: Ch3, 2dc in first st, 2dc, *ch1, sk 1 st, 1dc* to last 2 sts, 1dc, 2dc in final st, turn. (67) sts

Row 18: Ch3, 2dc in first st, 1dc, *ch1, sk 1 st, 1 dc* to last st, 2dc in final st, turn. (69) sts

Row 19: Rep Row 17. (71) sts

Row 20: Rep Row 16. (73) sts

Row 21: Ch3, 2dc in first st, 1dc, ch1, sk 1 st, 4dc, *ch1, sk 1 st, bobble, ch1, sk 1 st, 4dc*, to last 3 sts, ch1, sk 1 st, 1dc, 2dc in final st, turn. (75) sts

Row 22: Rep Row 16. (77) sts

Fasten off, leaving a long tail.

Sizes (3X, 4X) only:

Rows 11–14: Rep Rows 5–8.

Row 15: Ch3, 2dc in first st, 1dc, *ch1, sk 1 st, bobble, ch1, sk 1 st, 4dc*, to last 5 sts, ch1, sk 1 st, bobble, ch1, sk 1 st, 1dc, 2dc in final st, turn. (65, 65) sts

Row 16: Ch3, 2dc in first st, 1dc in each st to last st, 2dc in final st, turn. (67, 67) sts

Row 17: Ch3, 2dc in first st, 1dc, *ch1, sk 1 st, 1dc* to last st, 2dc in final st, turn. (69, 69) sts

Row 18: Ch3, 2dc in first st, *ch1, sk 1 st, 1dc* to last 2 sts, ch1, sk 1 st, 2dc in final st, turn. (71, 71) sts

Row 19: Rep Row 17. (73, 73) sts

Row 20: Rep Row 16. (75, 75) sts

Row 21: Ch3, 2dc in first st, *ch1, sk 1 st, bobble, ch1, sk 1 st, 4dc* to last 4 sts, ch1, sk 1 st, bobble, ch1, sk 1 st, 2dc in final st, turn. (77, 77) sts

Row 22: Rep Row 16. (79, 79) sts

Row 23: Ch3, 2dc in first st, 1dc, *ch1, sk 1 st, 1dc* to last st, 2dc in final st, turn. (81, 81) sts

Row 24: Ch3, 2dc in first st, *ch1, sk 1 st, 1dc* to last 2 sts, ch1, sk 1 st, 2dc in final st, turn. (83, 83) sts

Row 25: Ch3, 2dc in first st, 1dc, *ch1, sk 1 st, 1dc* to last 1dc in final st, turn. (84, 84) sts

Row 26: Ch3, 1dc in each st.

Fasten off, leaving a long tail.

Size (5X) only

Row 11: Rep Row 5.

Row 12: Ch3, 2dc in first st, 1dc, *ch1, sk 1 st, 1dc* to last st, 2dc in final st, turn. (65) sts

Row 13: Ch3, 2dc in first st, *ch1, sk 1 st, 1 dc* to last 2 sts, ch1, sk 1 st, 2dc in final st, turn. (67) sts

Row 14: Ch3, 2dc in first st, 1dc in each st to last st, 2dc in final st, turn. (69) sts

Row 15: Ch3, 2dc in first st, 4dc, *ch1, sk 1 st, bobble, ch1, sk 1 st, 4dc* to last st, 2dc in final st, turn. (71) sts

Row 16: Rep Row 14. (73) sts

Row 17: Ch3, 2dc in first st, *ch1, sk 1 st, 1 dc* to last 2 sts, ch1, sk 1 st, 2dc in final st, turn. (75) sts

Row 18: Ch3, 2dc in first st, 1dc, *ch1, sk 1 st, 1dc* to last st, 2dc in final st, turn. (77) sts

Row 19: Rep Row 17. (79) sts

Row 20: Rep Row 14. (81) sts

Row 21: Ch3, 2dc in first st, 3dc, *ch1, sk 1 st, bobble, ch1, sk 1 st, 4dc*, to last 7 sts, ch1, sk 1 st, bobble, ch1, sk 1 st, 3dc, 2dc in final st, turn. (83) sts

Row 22: Rep Row 14. (85) sts

Row 23: Ch3, 2dc in first st, *ch1, sk 1 st, 1 dc* to last 2 sts, ch1, sk 1 st, 2dc in final st, turn. (87) sts

Row 24: Ch3, 2dc in first st, 1dc, *ch1, sk 1 st, 1dc* to last st, 2dc in final st, turn. (89) sts

Row 25: Ch3, 2dc in first st, *ch1, sk 1 st, 1 dc* to last 2 sts, ch1, sk 1 st, 2dc in final st, turn. (91) sts

Row 26: Ch3, 1dc in each st.

Fasten off, leaving a long tail.

Finishing

With RS tog and using long yarn tails, seam shoulders by joining 14 (16, 19, 22) (25, 28, 31) (34, 37, 40) sts from outer edge of Front Panels with same number of sts on Back Panel.

Join Sleeve seam using long yarn tails.

Seam sides and join Sleeves to body.

Neckline edging

Using 6mm (US size J/10) hook and with RS facing, join yarn in any st at back of neckline.

Round 1: Ch1, loosely ss in each st around entire neckline, ss in ch-1 to join.

Fasten off.

GENERAL TECHNIQUES

Stitches

Slip knot

This knot attaches the yarn to the hook. Make a loop in the yarn near the end, leaving a tail of about 15cm (6in) (**1**). With your fingers or the hook, grab the ball-end of the yarn and draw it through the loop to the front (**2**). Pull both ends of the yarn to secure the knot around the hook. Do not pull too tightly, leave the slip knot slightly loose on the hook (**3**).

Chain (ch)

Begin with a slip knot on the hook. Hold the hook in your dominant hand and the base of the slip knot with the left thumb and forefinger of the other hand. Take the working yarn over the hook – abbreviated as yo (**4**) – twist the hook counterclockwise to catch the yarn (**5**) and pull it through the slip knot to create a new chain stitch (**6**). Continue until you have the required number of chain stitches, gently pulling down on the chain as you go.

Back loop only (BLO)

To work a stitch back loop only, insert the hook into the back loop of the next stitch (**7**), the loop furthest from you, instead of into both loops at the top of the stitch

Front loop only (FLO)

To work a stitch front loop only, insert the hook into the front loop of the next stitch (**8**), the loop nearest to you, instead of into both loops at the top of the stitch.

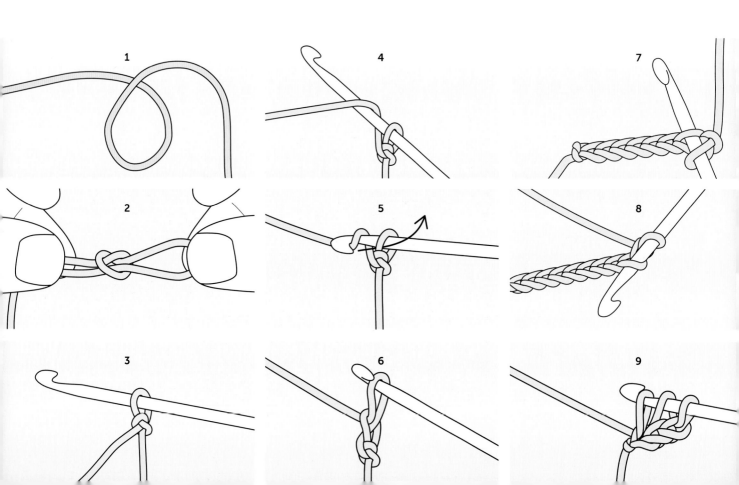

Foundation double crochet (fdc)

Make a slip knot on your hook, chain 3, yarn over, insert the hook into the third chain from the hook, yarn over, pull through the chain **(9)**, yarn over, pull through 1 loop on the hook (this creates your next chain), [yarn over, pull through 2 loops on the hook] twice **(10)**. *yarn over, insert the hook into the chain just made **(11)**, yarn over, pull through the chain, yarn over,

pull through 1 loop on the hook (this creates your next chain), [yarn over, pull through 2 loops on the hook] twice **(12)**; rep from * to create as many stitches as required.

Single crochet (sc)

Insert the hook into the next stitch **(13)**, yarn over, pull through the stitch, yarn over and pull through both loops on the hook **(14)**.

Single crochet 2 stitches together (sc2tog)

[Insert the hook into the next stitch, yarn over, pull through the stitch] **(15)** twice, yarn over, pull through 3 loops on the hook **(16)**.

Double crochet (dc)

Yarn over, insert the hook into the next stitch, yarn over, pull through the stitch **(17)**, yarn over, pull through 2 loops on the hook **(18)**, yarn over, pull through both loops on the hook to complete the stitch.

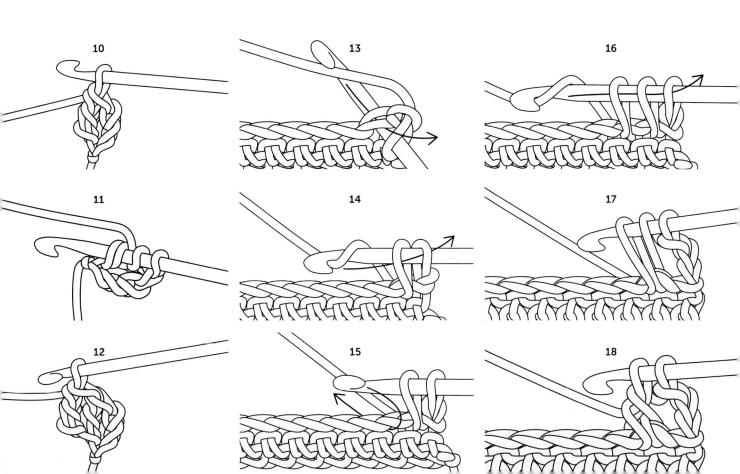

Crossed double crochet

Skip 1 stitch, 1dc into the next stitch, then working in front of the stitch just made, 1dc in the skipped stitch.

Double crochet 2 stitches together (dc2tog)

[Yarn over, insert the hook into the next stitch, yarn over, pull through the stitch, yarn over, pull through 2 loops on the hook (**1**)] twice, yarn over, pull through 3 loops on the hook (**2**).

Half double crochet (hdc)

Yarn over, insert the hook into the next stitch (**3**), yarn over, pull through the stitch (**4**), yarn over, pull through all 3 loops on the hook.

Slip stitch (ss)

Insert the hook into the next stitch, yarn over (**5**), pull through the stitch, pull the first loop on the hook through the second loop on the hook to complete the stitch (**6**).

Front post double crochet (FPdc)

Yarn over, insert the hook behind the post of the next stitch (**7**), yarn over and pull around the stitch (**8**), [yarn over, pull through 2 loops on the hook] twice.

Back post double crochet (BPdc)

This is worked in the same way as front post double crochet, except you begin by inserting the hook in front of the post of the next stitch.

Bead stitch

Skip 1 stitch, 1dc in the next stitch, [yarn over, insert the hook behind the post of the dc just made, yarn over and pull around the stitch] three times (**9**), yarn over, pull through 5 loops on the hook, yarn over, pull through 2 remaining loops on the hook (**10**).

Bobble

The instructions here are for a 3-dc bobble; to work a 4-dc bobble repeat the instruction in square brackets four times.

[Yarn over, insert the hook into the stitch, yarn over, pull through the stitch, yarn over, pull through 2 loops on the hook] three times (**11**), yarn over, pull through all remaining loops on the hook (**12**).

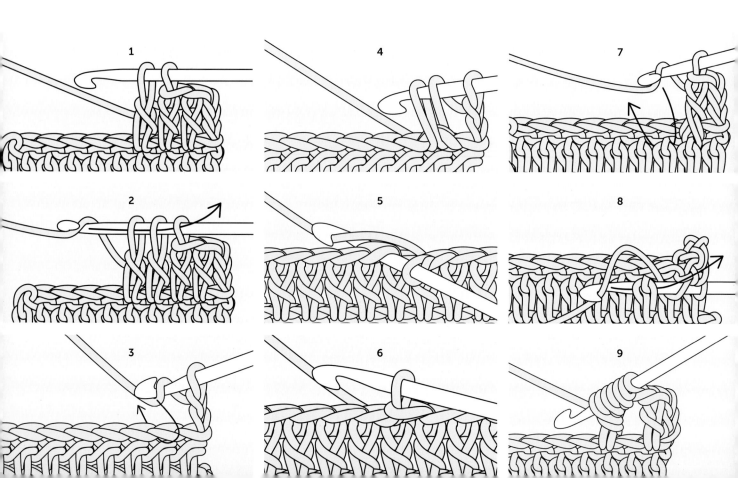

Finishing

Seaming

Lay your body panels flat with RS facing. Lay the sleeve next to the body panels, making sure the seam is at the underarm. Place a marker where the base of the sleeve meets the body panels **(13)**. Seam the sides, either by sewing or by working 2sc through each row end up to the marker, then continue to seam the sleeve in the same way. It helps to use markers to join the sleeve to the body panels to keep it in position.

Blocking

It's always a good idea to block your work once it's finished. It helps even out all the stitches and gives your garment extra pizzazz! I prefer to use the steam blocking method as follows:

Lay the garment down on a soft, flat surface. I use foam flooring mats, but you could use a yoga mat, the carpet in a low foot traffic room, or even your mattress. Use blocking pins to pin the garment out to the dimensions given in the pattern, then gently steam it all over with a handheld steam iron. Once dry just unpin your make and you're good to go.

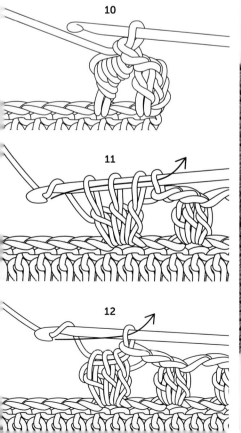

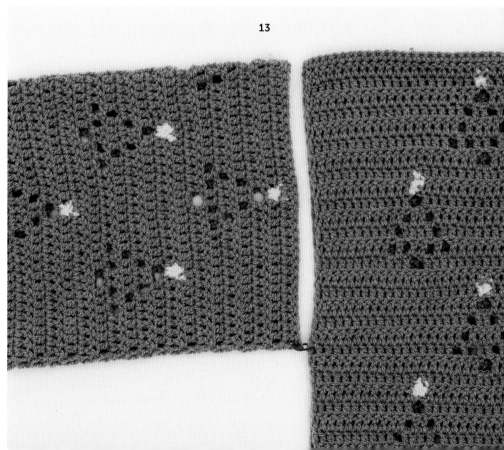

About the
AUTHOR

Lauren lives in Gravesend, UK, with her husband Matt and their two lurchers, Wally and Romy. She is the maker of spreadsheets behind all of the @manatee_squares patterns, a dedicated follower of loungewear, and a committed (if not necessarily successful) cultivator of houseplants.

T H A N K S

Thanks to my husband Matt Fagan for always supporting my questionable career decisions and to my dogs for being my constant crochet companions.

Thanks to my family for their continued enthusiasm every time I show them a new make, particularly my nephew George for his unmatched dedication to the Manatee Squares brand.

A huge shout out to my tip top gang of testers for spotting all my silly mistakes and helping me make my patterns legible for people other than myself.

And thanks to everyone at David & Charles who put their faith in my patterns and made this book the piece of art that it is.

Suppliers

YARN:
Paintbox Yarns, LoveCrafts
www.lovecrafts.com

HOOKS:
Cupcake Crochet Crafts
@cupcake_crochet_crafts
www.etsy.com/shop/cupcakecrochetcrafts

INDEX

A DAVID AND CHARLES BOOK
© David and Charles, Ltd 2024

David and Charles is an imprint of David and Charles, Ltd
Suite A, Tourism House, Pynes Hill, Exeter, EX2 5WS

A catalogue record for this book is available from the British Library.

ISBN-13: 9781446310649 paperback
ISBN-13: 9781446312049 EPUB
ISBN-13: 9781446312216 PDF

This book has been printed on paper from approved suppliers and made from pulp from sustainable sources.

Printed in China through Asia Pacific Offset for:
David and Charles, Ltd
Suite A, Tourism House, Pynes Hill, Exeter, EX2 5WS

10 9 8 7 6 5 4 3 2 1

Publishing Director: Ame Verso
Senior Commissioning Editor: Sarah Callard
Managing Editor: Jeni Chown
Editor: Jessica Cropper
Project Editor: Marie Clayton
Head of Design: Anna Wade
Designers: Jess Pearson and Tessa Sanders-Barwick
Pre-press Designer: Susan Reansbury
Illustrations: Kuo Kang Chen
Art Direction: Sarah Rowntree
Photography: Jason Jenkins
Production Manager: Beverley Richardson

David and Charles publishes high-quality books on a wide range of subjects. For more information visit **www.davidandcharles.com**.

Share your makes with us on social media using #dandcbooks and follow us on Facebook and Instagram by searching for @dandcbooks.

Layout of the digital edition of this book may vary depending on reader hardware and display settings.

There is an additional project available to download from www.bookmarkedhub.com. Search for this book by the title or ISBN: the file can be found under 'Book Extras'. Membership of the Bookmarked online community is free.